Extraordinary Young People

Extraordinary Young People

BY
MARLENE TARG BRILL

Children's Press©
A Division of Scholastic Inc.
New York Toronto London Auckland Sydney
Mexico City New Delhi Hong Kong
Danbury, Connecticut

Acknowledgments

The author wishes to thank the following organizations and individuals for their assistance to research for this book: Australian Consulate-General, New York, NY; The Cousteau Society, Norfolk, Virginia; Historical Society of Douglas County, Omaha, Nebraska; Lake County Museum, Wauconda, Illinois; Little League Baseball, Inc., Williamsport, Pennsylvania; Ray C. Leonard, Bethesda, Maryland; National Boy Scouts of America, Irving, Texas; Maria Mitchell Museum, Nantucket, Massachusetts; Pony Express Museum, St. Joseph, Missouri; Samantha Smith Foundation, Hallowell, Maine; United States Committee for UNICEF, New York and Chicago.

Photo Credits

Front Cover: UPI/Bettman (left, and wrap to back cover); SuperStock International (right, top); AP/Wide World (right, bottom)
Back Cover: UPI/Bettmann (left, top); ©Walter Scott (left, bottom)
5, ©1988 Stephen Ellison/*PEOPLE Weekly*; 8 (top, left), ©Walter Scott; 8 (top, second from left), AP/Wide World; 8 (top, second from right), SuperStock International; 8 (top, right; bottom), UPI/Bettmann; 10, Bettmann; 13, 15, 17, Stock Montage, Inc.; 19, 20, North Wind Picture Archive; 23, Stock Montage, Inc.; 26, North Wind; 28, AP/Wide World; 29, Gannett Newspapers; 32, 35, AP/Wide World; 36, Stock Montage, Inc.; 39, North Wind; 42, Stock Montage, Inc.; 46, Bettmann; 50, Stock Montage, Inc.; 53, AP/Wide World; 54, 57, Bettmann; 59, 60, North Wind; 62, 65, Bettmann; 66, UPI/Bettmann; 70, 73, Stock Montage, Inc.; 74, Courtesy "The President's Own" United States Marine Band; 76, AP/Wide World; 78, 80, 81, UPI/Bettmann; 83, AP/Wide World; 85, UPI/Bettmann; 87, 88, AP/Wide World, 90, Bettmann; 92, UPI/Bettmann; 95, Bettmann; 98, AP/Wide World; 101; UPI/Bettmann; 103, SuperStock International; 104 (top), Bettmann; 104 (bottom), UPI/Bettmann; 105, 106, 108, AP/Wide World; 111, courtesy Ruth Duskin Feldman; 114, AP/Wide World; 116, UPI/Bettmann; 117, 119, 121, AP/Wide World; 123, 124, UPI/Bettmann; 125 (both photos), 126, 127 (bottom), AP/Wide World; 127 (top), UPI/Bettmann; 128, courtesy Viking Press; 131, 135, 136, AP/Wide World; 138, UPI/Bettmann; 139, 141, 142, 145, AP/Wide World; 146, ©Walter Scott; 148; courtesy Youth ALIVE!; 152, 155, ©North Wind; 156, UPI/Bettmann; 159, courtesy John C. Wait; 162, ©1988 Stephen Ellison/*PEOPLE Weekly*; 165, ©Carol Rosegg; 167, AP/Wide World; 168, courtesy Atlantic Recording Corporation; 169, Mike Jones/Qwest; 170 (both photos), UPI/Bettmann; 171, 172 (both photos), 173 (top), AP/Wide World; 173 (bottom), Movie Still Archives; 174, AP/Wide World; 175, Lon Cooper/*The Dallas Morning News*; 178, Kaz Tsuruta/©1990 Asian Art Museum; 181, ©Alan Levenson/AllSport USA; 183, Bettmann; 184, UPI/Bettmann; 187, courtesy *Daily Globe*; 190, Reuters/Bettmann; 194, courtesy the United States Chess Federation

Library of Congress Cataloging-in-Publication Data

Brill, Marlene Targ.
    Extraordinary young people / by Marlene Targ Brill.
      p. cm. — (Extraordinary people) Includes bibliographical references and index.
    Summary: Biographical accounts of remarkable individuals in history who achieved noteworthy goals at an early age, from young warrior and Mongol leader Genghis Khan to nine-year-old chess champion Nawrose Nur.
    ISBN 0-516-00587-1 (lib. bdg.) — ISBN 0-516-26044-8 (pbk.)
    1. Gifted children—Biography—Juvenile literature. [1. Gifted children.] I. Title. II. Series

CT107.B66 1996   91-35175
920'.0087'9—dc20 [B]   CIP AC r95

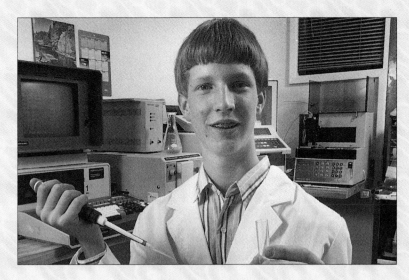

CONTENTS

PREFACE

History books reveal a host of stories about the great deeds of men and women. Few texts, however, describe the countless contributions made by children. Without the talent and daring of youth, modern society would be a much different place. Extraordinary Young People *celebrates the accomplishments and special talents of young children and teenagers in many eras.*

Different societies have assigned varying roles to children. Within similar cultures, new generations of adults treat their children differently. Some adults grant their children's every wish, while some parents restrict their children, controlling what they say and do. And while some parents take special care in guiding and educating their children, others mistreat and even abuse their offspring.

One fact, however, has remained constant since the beginning of time. Children continually prove that they have the resources to rise above the most difficult situations. As a group, children possess the abilities to excel in scientific invention, artistic creation, and heroism in the face of danger.

The boys and girls profiled in these pages were chosen because they acted in ways that were extraordinary for their young ages, in their cultures, and in their eras. These young people made their marks in history by the age of seventeen—some as early as age three! More than fifty people are described, representing youth from the eleventh century to the late twentieth century.

Many famous people, such as Thomas Edison, Rachel Carson, and Judy Garland, are portrayed here. But many other "ordinary" children are included as well; they displayed courage, daring, and endurance in more everyday endeavors, and their fame was not so widespread. Several faced harsh parents, poverty, war, or a variety of other handicaps, so their achievements merit inclusion in this collection alongside monumental geniuses. All of these young people, famous or not, inspire us to follow their examples.

— Marlene Targ Brill

TEMUJIN (GENGHIS KHAN)
LEADER AND WARRIOR AT AGE NINE
CA. 1162–1227

About eight hundred years ago, nomad tribes roamed the rugged steppe of central Asia. Tribespeople lived as herders on the untamed mountains and grasslands of the Gobi desert. Both adults and children tamed wild horses and carved bows and arrows for protection and hunting. Because the weather was harsh, tribal chieftains moved their herds with the seasons for better grazing. As they migrated, tribes frequently waged war on settlements in their paths. Tribal warfare and changing alliances were the core of steppe life. That is how Temujin became Borjigin Mongol chief at age nine and began showing skill as an exceptionally cunning warrior.

When Temujin was born, his father, Yesugei, was Borjigin Mongol chief of forty thousand tents. Yesugei was considered a brave lord who sought to unify steppe tribes under his banner of the nine yak tails. According to Mongol custom, a newborn child was to receive a name representing the family's most important recent event. The day of his first-born's birth,

Yesugei had just returned from winning a battle against a Tatar chieftain. Yesugei named his son Temujin after the captured chief.

Legend recounts that the baby was born with a large, red blood clot in his hand. The superstitious Mongols believed this mark foretold the boy's destiny to become a great conqueror. They did not know then that Temujin would fulfill this prediction at an unusually early age.

As was the custom when a boy turned nine, Temujin's father took him to another tribe to find a bride. Yesugei left his son in the future bride's camp to get to know her tribespeople. On the way back, Yesugei was poisoned by enemy Tatars who recognized him as their enemy. By the time Temujin received the news, his father was dead.

Yesugei's followers began leaving the Mongol camp in great numbers. The warriors doubted they would be safe with a nine-year-old boy as leader. Rather than rally around Temujin, most tribesmen rejected the youth's authority and abandoned his family to die at the hands of the dead chief's enemies, who would seek revenge on the children. Temujin resolved that the family should remain on his father's pasture. He would be the new chief.

The first enemies came at night. They rode into camp looking for red-headed Temujin and shooting fiery arrows into the felt tents that Mongols used for homes. Temujin gathered the children to flee across the river. To trick the enemy, he sent the children in different directions. Temujin fled into the hills, where he stayed for days without food. When the hungry boy stole down the hill, the enemy captured him and took him to their camp. They restrained him with a heavy wooden yoke around his neck and wrists. Temujin escaped after many days. A kind stranger helped him out of the yoke.

Temujin searched for his mother, brothers and sisters, and the few men who still served his family. Instead of seeking shelter with a friendly chieftain, the proud lad chose to keep the remains of his tribe on their own land. To survive, Temujin and his small following fished and hunted. The young chief claimed the same taxes, in the form of animals, that were once owed to his father.

Some warriors obeyed and then tried to steal the animals back. They found it strange to pay taxes to a youngster who could not defend them. Still, Temujin insisted that he was their *khan*, or chief. He reacted with great strength to their tricks. Every clash showed his uncommon wisdom and extraordinary skill in battle.

Slowly, Temujin gained a loyal following among younger Mongol warriors. At age seventeen, Temujin felt he had enough strength to claim some of his father's friends as allies. His first request was to the chieftain who had promised his daughter as bride. After considerable feasting on milk, wine, and meat, Temujin rode off with his new wife.

In the winter, Temujin led his people through unfriendly territory toward more fertile pastures. By now, the teenager commanded an army that was thirteen thousand strong. But their number was not as great as the thirty thousand who swooped down on them. Quickly, Temujin sprang into action. He divided his army into regiments. One after the other, the regiments attacked in waves of great force. Within a short time, Temujin's warriors had killed six thousand men and scared off the rest. News of the heroic victory over an army more than twice as strong spread throughout the steppe. Rumors declared that young Temujin had power from the gods.

With each brave act, Temujin gained followers. He initiated raids, treaties, and marriages to regain his family's position among steppe tribes. He gradually became the unchallenged leader of the Borjigin Mongols. In 1206, Temujin assembled a *Kuriltai*, or Great Council, to choose one ruler over Asia. Temujin became Genghis Khan, "Supreme Ruler of the Ocean."

The same persistence that saved young Temujin from his father's enemies drove Genghis Khan to create the most powerful organization of nations under a single ruler.

JOAN OF ARC
PATRIOT AND HEROINE AT AGE SEVENTEEN
1412–1431

The French kingdom was in turmoil in 1429. War had persisted between France and England for nearly a century. England now occupied land to the north including Rheims, the city where French kings were crowned. Charles, the true heir to the throne, was unable to become king. French nobility split between those who claimed the royal throne for Charles, and the Burgundians, who conspired with the English. In desperation, superstitious country folk clung to the hope that the wizard Merlin's prophecy would come true. A maid in men's clothing from the Lorraine district was to save France and restore the crown to a French king. That maid turned out to be Joan of Arc, a girl of seventeen.

Joan of Arc was born in Domremy, a small farm village on the border of Lorraine province. She lived a peasant's life with her father Jacques d'Arc, mother Isabellette, sister, and three brothers. Joan guided animals to pasture by day and helped her mother weave at night. Like most farm children of the day, Joan was uneducated, hardworking, and religious.

As Joan grew older, her belief in God deepened. She prayed for hours in the nearby church. As other girls offered flowers to fairies in a game, Joan made offerings to the saints.

One afternoon, Joan heard voices in her father's garden. To her surprise, the sounds appeared to come from a brilliant light she saw. From this light, Joan believed she saw Archangel Michael. He told her to pray and lead a good life, for she was to have a mission from God. Her job was to bring the future king to Rheims to be crowned. Then she was to drive the English from France. When Joan asked how a mere girl could do such deeds, the answer she heard was, "God will help thee."

As years passed, Joan saw more frequent visions of St. Michael, St. Catherine, and St. Margaret. When she was sixteen, she heard the voices more frequently. English troops were poised to attack Orleans. If the city fell, the voices cautioned, all France was lost to the English and Burgundians.

Joan went to one of Charles's loyal nobles and asked him for a horse, armor, and safe passage to the future king. At first, the officer resisted the thought of a peasant girl leading troops to save France. Even the idea of a girl wearing men's clothing was outrageous.

Joan persisted. She returned several times to press her case. Between visits, she told villagers how she would save the kingdom. Before long, townspeople and nobles, alike, believed in Joan. Finally, the officer approved her journey.

News of the brave girl reached the uncrowned king's court. Charles's attendants were unsure whether they should allow Joan to enter. When word of the attack on Orleans reached the desperate ruler, he decided to meet this self-proclaimed messenger from God.

Joan had claimed that because of her visions, she would be able to recognize the king, even though she had never seen him. So he dressed as an attendant to test her claim. When Joan entered his court, she immediately spotted Charles in a large crowd and knelt before him.

Despite her recognition of Charles, his advisers refused to believe Joan. They persuaded Charles to have Joan tested by scholars. They would determine whether she was from God, as she claimed, or a witch from the devil. After weeks of questioning, Joan's straightforward, intelligent answers convinced the scholars. She earned the right to continue her mission.

Joan took her place at the head of her troops dressed in heavy armor and a steel cap. She left her face visible so the soldiers could be inspired by her lead in battle. In her hand, Joan carried a white banner embroidered with Jesus's image and the names of Jesus and Mary. The sight of this determined girl in a man's uniform gave the soldiers new hope and courage.

Legend explains how mysterious voices directed Joan to attack and win in battle. She led her troops against several English forts that surrounded Orleans. During one battle, an arrow wounded her. She pulled it from her body, went off to pray for guidance, and returned as a supreme inspiration to her troops.

As the English fled, people of Orleans were convinced that a miracle was taking place. A seventeen-year-old girl who had never held a sword succeeded where military experts had failed. Uplifted by victory and Joan's presence, the army pushed the English northward until they reopened the road to Rheims. Three months later, Joan proudly took her place with Charles VII at his formal coronation as king of France.

Joan wanted to press toward Paris and force the English from France. However, the weak king refused to lend support to her plans. The Burgundians and English, in addition to many of the king's nobles and priests, were fearful and jealous of her power. Instead, Charles secretly planned a treaty with the Burgundians to keep a shaky peace.

Unable to remain still, Joan assembled four hundred men and entered the occupied town of Compiègne. This time, the battle went badly. Joan was captured and delivered to the English. Charles refused to admit that he owed his crown to Joan and did nothing to free her.

The English kept Joan of Arc chained in a dark, damp cell for six months before her trial. She was tried as a heretic, someone who refuses to follow church teachings. Clergy charged that the voices she heard were the result of witchcraft. But Joan believed that the voices sustained her through her imprisonment. On May 30, 1431, Joan of Arc was burned at the stake at Rouen. As fire blazed around her, onlookers wept, believing that they were burning a saint. But the story of the brave young girl who saved France would not die. Nineteen years later, a new trial cleared Joan's name. Centuries later, in 1920, the Roman Catholic Church declared Joan of Arc a saint. She would be remembered in church lore for following heavenly voices of her youth to victory.

MICHELANGELO BUONARROTI
FAMOUS ARTIST AT AGE FIFTEEN
1475–1564

On April 1, 1488, Lodovico Buonarroti reluctantly signed a contract binding his son Michelangelo to artists Domenico and David Ghirlandaio for three years. This contract made thirteen-year-old Michelangelo the happiest boy in Florence. Now he could be an artist. He could begin his life's work.

Michelangelo always had dreamed of being a sculptor, and sculpting had seemed his destiny. As an infant, Michelangelo's mother was unable to nurse him. She sent the baby to a stonecutter's wife in a hilltop village for feeding. Later, Michelangelo joked that the milk he drank "was mixed with marble dust, which led to a lifelong passion for marble."

Michelangelo's mother often was sick or too weak to care for him and his four brothers. She died when he was six. For the next four years, Michelangelo lived with the stonecutters. Rather than learning to read and write like other Florentine boys, Michelangelo learned to handle a hammer and chisel. He loved the feeling of smooth stone. When he studied a piece of rock, he almost could see human forms that were trying to break free. The boy longed to learn how to help those figures come to life.

When Michelangelo was ten, his father remarried. Michelangelo returned to Florence and entered grammar school. Although he stayed three years, the boy hated school and never felt at home in his father's house. His father disapproved of art, thinking artists were beneath the family's place in Italian society.

Michelangelo found comfort and freedom in drawing. He sought the company of other boys who were interested in art. An older boy named Granacci befriended him. Granacci was an apprentice at the art studio of the well-known Ghirlandaio brothers. As apprentice, Granacci learned a trade in exchange for performing menial tasks. Granacci showed the great artist Domenico Ghirlandaio some of Michelangelo's work. Ghirlandaio was so impressed that he decided to hire Michelangelo as an apprentice.

Michelangelo had an uncommonly good memory for art. He easily mastered art techniques such as fresco (painting on damp plaster), sculpture, and sketching. He was clearly more talented than the older boys at the studio.

Ghirlandaio was impressed by Michelangelo's remarkable ability. On one occasion, Michelangelo changed a figure in a fresco drawing without permission. Ghirlandaio became enraged that Michelangelo would correct a master. Then he realized that Michelangelo's change was for the best, and he left it on the painting.

During the fourteenth and fifteenth centuries, art flourished in Italy. Families with great wealth supported painters, sculptors, and architects. Lorenzo de Medici, of the wealthy ruling Florentine family, requested two of Ghirlandaio's best students to attend his new sculpture studio. Ghirlandaio recommended Michelangelo and Granacci. Michelangelo was overjoyed. He spent his days eagerly studying the wonderful figures Lorenzo displayed in the Medici sculpture garden and learning how to carve stone and mold clay.

Lorenzo invited the gifted fifteen-year-old to become his personal artist. Michelangelo left his father's run-down house and moved into a private, deluxe room in the Medici palace. Lorenzo and his sons granted Michelangelo honors normally given to the most gifted, long-standing artists of state.

Michelangelo pursued his love for art until he died at age ninety. During that time he created some of the world's greatest masterpieces. The boy who sought to free figures from marble became one of the most famous artists of his day—and perhaps the finest artist ever.

— A statue of Michelangelo —

BENJAMIN WEST
ARTIST AT AGE SIX
1738–1820

Benjamin West's mother discovered her son's artistic talent accidentally. Mrs. West asked Benjamin to watch his sister's sleeping baby while the two women gathered flowers. Benjamin agreed, hoping the baby would awaken soon so that they could play. As time passed, however, an unusual feeling overcame seven-year-old Benjamin. He was so charmed by the baby's smile that he picked up a pen and drew a picture of the child.

As his mother and sister approached, Benjamin tried to hide the drawing. The Wests were strict Quakers, and Quakers did not approve of drawing likenesses of people. But when Mrs. West noticed the paper and asked to see it, the boy showed it to her.

To her surprise, Benjamin had made an exact likeness of the baby. Mrs. West kissed her son proudly and wonderd how he had learned to draw. She knew that traveling artists stayed away from Springfield Township, Pennsylvania, their Quaker community. To her knowledge, Benjamin had never in his life seen a painting. Benjamin told his mother that he was able to copy what he saw around him. He proceeded to draw the flowers his mother held. Mrs. West was so delighted that she showed the sketches to her husband. The Wests then encouraged Benjamin to explore his talent.

There was plenty to draw at the roadside inn where the family lived and worked. Wagonloads of farmers, merchants, and German immigrants stopped for food and lodging on their way east to Philadelphia. Between his chores of watering horses and filling warming pans with coals, Benjamin sketched birds and flowers from the countryside.

One day, Benjamin's drawing interested a group of American Indians who came to trade with the Quakers. As they watched Benjamin work with pen and ink, an Indian asked Benjamin why he never used colors. The boy explained that he had no color paints. The Indians showed Benjamin how to find yellow and red dirt and clay. Then they dried the dirt in the sun and mixed it with sticky sap from acacia trees so the paint would spread smoothly. When Benjamin told his mother what he had learned, Mrs. West offered some blue indigo dye that she used for cloth. Now Benjamin had red, yellow, and blue paint—the primary colors.

Helpful neighbors remarked that Benjamin still needed pencils in order to paint. "Pencils" in that time were bundles of camels' hair fastened in a quill. Since there were no camels in North America, Benjamin had to find something else. The creative youngster plucked fur from his father's favorite cat. As the quill needed more hair, the cat began to look ill. Luckily, Benjamin's father noticed the cat before it became bald.

When a cousin, Mr. Pennington, saw Benjamin's work, he was surprised he could draw so well with such crude materials. Pennington was a merchant in Philadelphia, and he sent Benjamin his first set of paints, brushes, and canvases. He also sent two etchings, the first artwork Benjamin had ever seen. Benjamin treasured the gift. He secretly stayed home from school to paint. By the time Mrs. West found out, Benjamin had painted a beautiful blending of the two engravings. In later years, Benjamin claimed that these early works were his best.

After seeing the fruits of his gifts, Mr. Pennington continued encouraging Benjamin's craft. With the Wests' consent, he took Benjamin to Philadelphia. There Benjamin met other artists for the first time, saw other pictures, and read whatever books he could find about art. The nine-year-old decided to become an artist.

News of the young, self-taught artist spread throughout the region. Many neighbors requested that Benjamin paint their portraits. By the time he was nineteen, Benjamin had established himself as a portrait painter in Philadelphia. He later went to New York where he met a wealthy merchant who offered him the opportunity to study in Italy, the art capital of the world. Benjamin became the first American painter to gain an art education abroad and to be accepted by Europeans. He was voted an honorary member of the art academies in Florence, Parma, and Bologna—a great honor for any artist. Benjamin later traveled to England, where he eventually was appointed historical painter for the king of England. He also was one of the original members of the Royal Academy.

During the years until his death at age eighty-two, Benjamin painted more than four hundred historical, religious, and portrait paintings for king George III. His scenic art signaled a new school of painting. Benjamin was the first artist to paint figures in their actual dress rather than in ancient Roman costume, as was the custom.

Benjamin's reputation spanned two continents. In England, he became known as the founder of historical painting. Americans remembered him as the young prodigy who represented the first glimmer of art in colonial North America.

PHILLIS WHEATLEY
POET AT AGE FIFTEEN
1753–1784

Should you, my lord, while you peruse my song,
Wonder from Whence my love of Freedom sprung,
Whence flow these wishes for the common good,
By feeling, fears alone best understood,
I, young in life, by seeming cruel fate
Was snatched from Africa's fancy'd happy seat. . . .
Such, such my case. And can I but pray
Others may never feel tyrannics way.

— Phillis Wheatley

A young African girl stood trembling on an auction platform. She was about eight years old, and she had just endured a long, horrible journey from her home in Africa. There, she had been kidnapped from her family to be sold at a slave market in a strange land.

Now she was in Boston, where colonists came from far away to buy and sell slaves. At the slave market, human beings were sold as if they were cattle or sheep.

Glaring eyes inspected the frightened child, who wore only a strip of soiled cloth. Susannah Wheatley and her merchant husband, John, spotted the girl. They thought she would be able to assist the elderly Mrs. Wheatley. Little did they know that their timid slave would blossom into a wonderful poet.

The Wheatleys named their new servant Phillis. Then they assigned their eighteen-year-old daughter, Mary, the task of teaching Phillis enough English to carry out her household chores. Phillis showed she was quick and intelligent, so Mary also taught her to read. In less than two years, Phillis became a skilled writer, and she could read the most complex sections of the Bible. Phillis eventually mastered grammar, mathematics, history, astronomy, and enough Greek and Latin to read the classics.

The Wheatleys soon realized that Phillis was unusually gifted. They decided to nurture her genius. Mrs. Wheatley relieved Phillis of some of her chores so that the girl could study. Phillis remained a slave, but the Wheatleys included her in family discussions and took her to the homes of many scholarly friends. Over the next few years, Phillis corresponded with noted colonists and dignitaries as far away as London. She also began expressing her thoughts in poetry.

In 1770, Phillis caused a stir in the colonies with the publication of her first poem. News of her remarkable talent spread quickly. Phillis's writing skills shocked those who believed that an African female teenager lacked normal intelligence and emotions.

As the years passed, Phillis's health weakened. Doctors suggested a sea cruise to improve her asthma, a condition that interferes with one's breathing. Mary's brother, Nathaniel, was about to depart for England on business, so the Wheatleys sent Phillis with him.

Phillis gained many admirers in England. Nobles found her a curiosity, being both an accomplished poet and an African-American slave. A woman named Lady Huntingdon arranged for the publication of a book of Phillis's poetry. Phillis was just under twenty years old when many famous colonists, including John Hancock, signed the foreword of her book, *Poems on Various Subjects, Religious and Moral*. Phillis became the first African-American woman ever to publish a book of verse.

Phillis's most notable poem was about the newly appointed commander of the colonial armies, George Washington. In "First in Peace," Phillis predicted that General Washington would free colonists from English tyranny and bring peace to the colonies. Washington was so touched by Phillis's writing that he took time to meet the young author.

In 1778, Phillis received her freedom after John Wheatley's death. But freedom brought uncertainty. Phillis had no home, few skills beyond writing, and limited physical strength. She married a free black man, but their marriage was plagued with problems. The couple had little money, and their first two children died as infants.

Phillis tried to earn money by publishing a volume of thirty-three poems. But at the height of the Revolutionary War, the public showed little interest in her tender, religious verse.

Phillis Wheatley died during the birth of her third baby on December 5, 1784. From her youth, she wrote about dreams of freedom, but Phillis never really experienced the liberty and happiness she imagined.

WOLFGANG AMADEUS MOZART
MUSICIAN AND COMPOSER AT AGE FOUR
1756–1791

here have been many gifted young musicians throughout history. But no child prodigy can match the genius of Wolfgang Amadeus Mozart.

Leopold Mozart, a composer and music instructor, first realized his son had extraordinary talents when the boy was barely four. The elder Mozart and a musician friend found the youngster writing at the clavier, a keyboard instrument. The two men wondered why the boy was so deep in thought. "I am composing a concerto, father," he said. Leopold examined the papers and handed them to his friend, Herr Schachtner. On the papers, Wolfgang had accurately written musical notes that seemed very difficult to play. The two men were even more dumbfounded when Wolfgang began to play the complicated piece just as it was written.

Leopold and his wife, Anna Maria, made music an important part of the household. Wolfgang and his older sister, Maria Anna, began music lessons as soon as they could reach the keyboard of the clavier. Maria Anna (or Nannerl, as she was called) was an excellent musician, but Wolfgang was in a class by himself. One day, Wolfgang listened to his father and his associates practicing a concerto. The men were then awestruck when the five-year-old repeated the violin part perfectly. He had memorized the music just by listening to the piece a single time!

Leopold wanted the world to know of his two prodigies. He set a rigid schedule of music study to prepare Nannerl and Wolfgang for public performances. The children did not play with other children outdoors. During free time, they practiced duets.

Because Leopold believed Wolfgang would be famous someday, he kept notes that detailed the boy's progress. Leopold taught his son clavier, violin, piano, and traditional school subjects. Certain parts of the day were devoted to practicing each instrument and to singing. Wolfgang also spent time composing his own music or copying masterpieces written by famous composers. As part of his bedtime routine, Wolfgang often made up songs of meaningless words. "Making music is the best fun in the world," he would say.

The first recitals Leopold arranged for Wolfgang and Nannerl were in or near Salzburg, Austria, their hometown. The children liked the attention and praise they received. Wolfgang earned the reputation as a *Wunderkind*, or "wonder child." Leopold decided that the children should perform for important people who could pay them large sums of money. Leopold had visions of becoming rich from the money his children could earn.

Wolfgang spent the rest of his childhood delighting audiences in palaces, concert halls, and churches throughout Europe. He and his sister played before kings, queens, and countless other dignitaries in such major cities as Frankfurt, Cologne, Brussels, Rome, Paris, and The Hague. In addition to playing serious music, Wolfgang impressed his audience with tricks, such as playing the piano with a cloth covering the keyboard, or using one finger instead of ten.

When he reached his teenage years, Wolfgang no longer attracted the attention he had drawn as a youngster. Now he performed alone because Nannerl was too old for a children's act. Wolfgang disliked his exhausting performance schedule and what he called "circus tricks." He wanted to be a serious musician, so he broke free from his father's control.

As a young adult, Wolfgang continued to compose music and give recitals and music lessons. He was continually plagued with money problems. Wolfgang wrote some of the world's greatest operas, symphonies, church music, and small-group concertos. Yet he lacked the bargaining skills to earn what his music was worth. Mozart died a pauper, leaving nothing but debts for his wife and two small children. He did, however, leave the world a wealth of the finest music ever written, some created when he was a little boy.

SYBIL LUDINGTON
REVOLUTIONARY WAR HERO AT AGE SIXTEEN
1761–1839

Sybil Ludington grew up during difficult times. In the 1770s, trouble was brewing between British colonists in North America and the king of England. England wanted to maintain tight control of the colonies, but colonists wanted to be free from British rule.

When fighting broke out between the colonists and British soldiers, Sybil's father had to leave home for war. Young Sybil, her mother, and her sister had to maintain the family gristmill and farm chores while he was gone. Sybil longed to play a role in the conflict. She wanted to help drive the British soldiers away.

Her chance came on April 26, 1777. On that cold, dark evening, Sybil made one of the most heroic rides of the American Revolution.

The previous year, the colonies had formally declared their independence from England. At that time, Sybil's father received a commission as colonel of the Seventh Militia of Dutchess County in New York. The British were creeping closer to the Ludingtons' hometown of Carmel, New York.

Colonel Ludington and his troops had to be prepared to go into battle at a moment's notice.

One night, Colonel Ludington was in his cabin when he heard rapid hoofbeats outside. A weary-looking rider burst into the room. In a frantic voice, he pleaded with the colonel to rouse his men for battle. British troops were raiding army storehouses less than 30 miles (48 km) away in Danbury, Connecticut. Unless they were stopped, the British would soon overrun Carmel.

Colonel Ludington knew that someone had to recall the men from their farms immediately. The messenger was too exhausted to make the long journey, and the colonel himself had to stay where he was to organize the troops as they arrived. Colonel Ludington was surprised when his daughter, Sybil, spoke up. She volunteered to ride out and alert the soldiers. At first, the two men refused the girl's offer. The ride was dangerous, particularly for a sixteen-year-old girl. Outlaws and army deserters lurked on country roads, ready to harm anyone crossing their path.

Sybil persisted. She knew where the soldiers lived, and she was a good rider. When Colonel Ludington finally agreed, Sybil raced for the barn. She mounted her horse, Star, and began the hazardous trip over the dark countryside.

Sybil sounded the alarm at each stop. Without dismounting, she called out that the British were burning Danbury. Men were to meet at her father's mill, and women were to prepare for a raid. As soon as someone acknowledged her message, Sybil rode to another farmhouse. She traveled to every farm in Carmel and then went to Lake Mahopac. By now, few lights burned. The hour was late, and the night grew chilly. The sky was black and threatening, and Sybil was having trouble finding her way in the dark. Just when she thought she was lost, lightning showed her the way.

Sybil pushed herself to ride all night. She traveled almost 40 miles (64 km) through thick woods and around rivers. At dawn, the breathless girl arrived back at home. Scores of men had gathered there, and they soon left for Danbury. Her job finished, Sybil at last climbed into bed.

The colonial troops arrived in time to block the British in Ridgefield, Connecticut. They surprised the enemy with such force that the British retreated to their ships.

News of Sybil's heroic ride spread. She was hailed as the "Female Paul Revere." Revere was the Boston messenger who, two years earlier, had warned people of a British attack. But Paul Revere was forty years old at the time of his ride. He rode only 16 miles (26 km), and he was ultimately captured! Sybil was sixteen years old, rode much farther, and completed her journey safely.

Sybil received many honors through the years. George Washington sent his personal thanks after the war. More recently, historic signs were placed to mark some of the stops along Sybil's dangerous route. In the 1970s, the U.S. Postal Service issued an eight-cent stamp showing Sybil and Star in action. Anna Hyatt Huntington sculpted a similar pose for her statue of Sybil and Star. The statue stands near the shore of Lake Gleneida in Carmel, New York, and a replica stands in downtown Danbury, Connecticut.

As an adult, Sybil married, raised six children, and cared for many more grandchildren. Two generations of youngsters never tired of hearing Sybil Ludington's story of her ride for freedom.

JOHN QUINCY ADAMS
FOREIGN DIPLOMAT AT AGE FOURTEEN
1767–1848

Abigail Adams urged her twelve-year-old son to accompany his father abroad. She told young John Quincy Adams that he was part of the "family destiny" to serve their country. His father, John Adams, already had sacrificed a profitable law practice to be a delegate of Massachusetts to the Continental Congress. Now Congress wanted the elder Adams to return to France on another diplomatic mission.

Young John Quincy Adams was fluent in French, and Abigail knew that his skill would be helpful to his father. But she could not predict that John Quincy would be called upon, at age fourteen, to represent his country as the first Russian ambassador's secretary.

John Quincy was born in Braintree, Massachusetts, a seaside farm village 9 miles (14 km) south of Boston. He was the second child and eldest son of Abigail and John Adams. At the time of John Quincy's birth, his father had played a leading role in promoting the American Revolution.

While his father defended colonial freedom, John Quincy remained at home to help his mother care for the other children and the farm. He assisted a hired worker in mending fences, driving the gravel cart, and planting crops. At night, John studied by candlelight in the kitchen. When full-scale war with England erupted, the local schools closed. Then Abigail supervised her son's study of history, writing, and religion. Her husband's law clerks taught the boy Latin and Greek.

War brought added burdens for the family, especially with John Adams so far away in Philadelphia. Many friends and relatives fled danger in Boston and settled in safer towns such as Braintree. Hungry troops passed through the community on the way to fight British Redcoats. There were many more mouths for the family to feed before the war ended. John Quincy Adams often stopped his chores and listened to cannons booming in nearby battlefields. He knew his time would come to serve his country in its struggle for independence.

After four years of service to the Continental Congress, John's father left Philadelphia to resume his law practice. The joy of having a father home again was short-lived. John Adams received orders to travel to France. Congress wanted the French to pledge support for the colonies against England.

John and Abigail decided that ten-year-old John Quincy could profit from a European education. In February 1778, young John and his father boarded the warship, *Boston*, bound for Europe. After a great storm, an attack by English pirates, and rough seas, the father and son arrived in France almost six weeks later.

John Adams settled his son at boarding school at Passy, a suburb of Paris, and went about his business. John Quincy Adams eagerly took to his studies of French, Latin, music, drawing, dancing, and fencing. John Adams wrote Abigail about how well John Quincy spoke French.

John Quincy stayed in Paris little more than a year. When his father's business ended, the two left for home in August 1779. John Quincy looked forward to finishing school in America and following his father's footsteps into Harvard Law School. But soon after John Quincy returned to Braintree, his father was recalled to Europe. This time, John Quincy wanted to stay home, but his strong-willed mother convinced him of his duty to family and country.

Once again, John Quincy studied at Passy Academy. When Congress ordered his father to Holland (The Netherlands), the thirteen-year-old transferred to Leiden University. He became one of the youngest boys to study at the famed European college. The move suited him well. In addition to his studies, the teenager enjoyed ice skating on Dutch canals during winter and riding horses past country windmills after the thaw. John Quincy found the refined European lifestyle a pleasant way to grow from a boy to a young man.

A year later, John Quincy received an opportunity that launched a lifetime of government service. Francis Dana became the first ambassador to Russia. The United States wanted Dana to negotiate a treaty with Czarina Catherine the Great. President George Washington believed that it was important for Russia to recognize the infant American government.

Ambassador Dana spoke no French, the diplomatic language at the Czarina's court. So fourteen-year-old John Quincy Adams accompanied Ambassador Dana to Russia as translator and interpreter. John Quincy became the first and only teenage foreign secretary to serve the United States.

John Quincy Adams traveled through Europe for more than a year before returning to Holland. In his travels, he received an education in diplomacy and communicating with people that could only be learned through experiences outside the classroom. These experiences, plus his eventual Harvard law degree, earned John Quincy Adams many government posts. He became minister to the Netherlands under his father, who by then was the second president of the United States. From there, he

— *John Quincy Adams* —

was elected to the United States Senate and was appointed ambassador to Russia and Great Britain. In 1817, President James Monroe appointed him secretary of state.

John Quincy Adams continued to follow his father's lifelong career in government. He was elected sixth president of the United States in 1824. Adams is the only son of a former president to be elected to the same office. After the presidency, he continued in government service as representative from his home district until his death at age eighty-one. He had fulfilled the strong sense of duty his parents had taught him at a very young age.

CARL FRIEDRICH GAUSS
MATH PRODIGY AT AGE THREE
1777–1855

Carl Friedrich Gauss was born to poor, uneducated parents in Brunswick, Germany. His father earned a meager living gardening, bricklaying, and doing odd jobs around town. He was an honest, stern man who had little use for education.

One day, Carl's father struggled to figure the payroll for his workers. Three-year-old Carl was supposed to be playing. Instead, he sat and listened to his father mumble totals for each column. Carl noticed that his father had made a mistake. The boy announced the correct sum aloud. He had computed the total in his head faster and more accurately than his father had on paper.

Even though Carl showed unusual talent, his father refused to send him to school. The custom in eighteenth-century Germany was for peasant boys to grow up learning their fathers' trades. But Carl's mother and uncle recognized the boy's quick mind and hoped he would achieve more than a peasant's life.

Carl's Uncle Johann was a weaver with an unusual variety of interests. The gentleman watched proudly as his nephew taught himself to read. Johann made sure that Carl had enough books to improve his mind. He spent time talking with young Carl and expanding his ideas.

Meanwhile, Carl's mother did what she could to encourage her son's studies when her stern husband was away. Carl's father of ten prohibited the boy from reading. He believed that Carl's studying by firelight drained the family's wood supply. When his father ordered him to bed, Carl carried a hard vegetable under his sleeve to hollow out and stuff with a cotton candlewick. He read for hours in the dim light from this makeshift candle.

Carl began formal schooling at age seven. His class was run by a harsh teacher, Herr Buttner, who frequently whipped students who disobeyed. When Carl was ten, Herr Buttner gave the class an assignment to complete within one hour. They were to write down all the numbers from one to one hundred; then they were to add them up and find their total. When the teacher completed the directions, he noticed that everyone was busy working except Carl. Herr Buttner grabbed his whip and stormed toward the trembling student.

Carl stammered as he told the teacher that he already had finished the problem. Herr Buttner took Carl's writing slate and found only one number written—5050. The teacher asked the boy how he arrived at the answer without writing down all the numbers. Carl explained that by adding numbers from opposite ends of the list, each pair equaled 101. For instance:

$$100 + 1 = 101$$
$$99 + 2 = 101$$
$$98 + 3 = 101$$

He realized that all 50 pairs in the sequence equaled 101. Therefore, he figured in his head:

$$50 \times 101 = 5050.$$

From that day on, Carl received private math instruction with Herr Buttner's assistant, Martin Bartels. Carl's math abilities blossomed under Bartels's guidance. Important townspeople began hearing about Carl's extraordinary mathematical skills.

On one occasion, the Duke of Brunswick summoned the boy to his palace. Carl's father was convinced that the visit was to scold the boy for reading in the palace gardens. Instead, the Duke wanted to see an example of the fourteen-year-old's accomplishments in person. Duke Ferdinand was so impressed with the bashful genius that he offered to be Carl's sponsor. The nobleman wanted to pay for Carl's education.

The next year Carl entered the Collegium Carolinum in Brunswick, a noted college preparatory school. Carl applied himself to the study of ancient and modern languages while pursuing advanced mathematical research. By the age of sixteen, he had discovered an alternative to Euclid's geometry. Within a year, he accurately criticized several theories that had been accepted for centuries.

In 1795, Carl left Brunswick for Germany's famous University of Gottingen. When he was eighteen, Carl discovered what is considered to be the greatest mathematical accomplishment of his career. Carl proved that a compass and a rule are all that are needed to construct a closed plane figure of seventeen sides.

By the end of his eighteenth year, his professors agreed that Carl had mastered the principles of the most outstanding mathematicians of the day. From these studies, the modest youth launched a significant career in mathematics. He later became a director at Gottingen, where he spent the rest of his life. In a short time, the boy who was once destined to remain a peasant became one of the top mathematicians of all time.

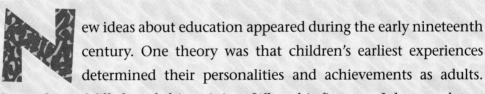

JOHN STUART MILL
STUDIED GREEK AT AGE THREE
PHILOSOPHER AS A TEENAGER
1806–1873

New ideas about education appeared during the early nineteenth century. One theory was that children's earliest experiences determined their personalities and achievements as adults. James Stuart Mill shared this opinion. When his first son, John, was born, James decided to raise him under the best learning conditions. He would teach John himself and mold the boy into a great philosopher.

John began studying Greek at age three and Latin at seven. From age six, the youngster was put through more than eight hours of tightly supervised study each day. He awoke at six in the morning and began two to three hours of instruction before breakfast.

After a thirty-minute meal, John resumed his work for another five hours. His father saved the most difficult lessons, such as arithmetic, for three-hour evening sessions.

Long walks with his father were John's only break from study. James used the time to talk about the books John had read the day before and to study nature. In their long discussions, James emphasized to his son that learning was more than just memorized facts. Often, James required his son to give written and verbal accounts of what they discussed on their walks.

John took to his studies eagerly. He was an avid reader who had a large share of youthful curiosity. Moreover, he had a strong desire to please his father, a severe taskmaster who prodded his son through history, drama, government, philosophy, and science.

By the age of eight, John was skilled enough in his studies to tutor his young brothers and sisters. In later years, John spent several hours every day giving many of them their only taste of education. James quizzed the children on the lessons that John taught. If the younger children were unable to answer any of James's questions, John was punished.

Throughout his childhood, John had no playthings. His only children's book was a single, beloved copy of *Robinson Crusoe*. Instead of playing with children his own age, John discussed politics and literature with adult friends of his father. James protected the boy from anything and anyone who might interfere with his learning progress.

By age twelve, John had completed classical readings normally tackled by university students in their late teens and twenties. Within two years, his formal education surpassed any twenty-five-year-old's. English scholars began noticing this remarkable youth.

Years of constant thoughtful discussion with James and his friends had laid the groundwork for skills in debate and writing. John later wrote that by the time he was fifteen, he had decided that his object in life was to be a world reformer. To this end, he formed a debating society to analyze philosophy, religion, and politics. He turned his early essays for his father into newspaper articles that were published for the entire community to read.

John grew more interested in politics, but his father had other goals for the teenager. At age seventeen, James gave John a job writing political letters and papers at the East India Company, where James worked. This highly respected government job brought John steady pay for the next thirty-five years. Equally important, the job left him plenty of time for study and writing.

Until his twentieth year, John never questioned his rigid, unfeeling upbringing or thought himself unusual. As an adult, he credited his merits to his father's belief in early learning. He claimed to be of average intelligence and memory. John remembers feeling ignorant because his father always was so annoyed with his work. But few ordinary children could have withstood the constant mental strain at so young an age.

Many educators claim that James's experiment was successful. John Stuart Mill became one of the most famous philosophers of the modern age. He produced scores of essays that changed the way people thought about politics and social life. To this day, John Stuart Mill's theories are taught in universities around the world.

LOUIS BRAILLE
INVENTED READING SYSTEM
FOR THE BLIND AT AGE FIFTEEN
1809–1852

The future was bleak for boys and girls of the early nineteenth century who were blind. Few schools or apprentice jobs were open to them. Blind children had no way to read and write or learn a trade. As adults, blind people often filled poorhouses or were locked away in institutions because they could not earn a living. Those who roamed the streets either became beggars or performed lowly farm and factory jobs in exchange for food and shelter. But Louis Braille decided that his life would be different. He wanted to read.

When he was born, Louis could see normally, like his four older siblings. The five children lived with their parents in the French village of Coupvray, east of Paris. Louis and his family shared the regular farm chores of harvesting grapes and vegetables, tending to the cows and chickens, and preparing meals. Most of all, little Louis liked watching his father make harnesses and saddles. His father gave him scraps of leather to play with, but he instructed Louis never to touch the sharp tools in the workshop. Most days, Louis was satisfied to play with these scraps. He pretended that they were soldiers from the French emperor's army.

One day, Louis grew tired of his leather soldiers. As his father was busy, the boy decided to make a harness by himself. Louis poked at the leather with an awl—a long, pointed tool for punching holes in leather. As the three-year-old stabbed at the leather, the tool slipped and its point punctured his left eye.

Louis's parents ran to the screaming boy. They bathed his eye and rushed him to the doctor. The doctor said little could be done except to bandage the injured eye. In the days ahead, Louis's eye became infected. Without the benefit of modern medicine, the infection spread to the other eye. Louis eventually recovered from the infection, but he was left blind in both eyes.

At first, the boy was too young to grasp what had happened. Louis asked his parents when daylight would reappear. The darkness made him bump into furniture and walls. He wanted to do more for himself. Louis's parents agreed that he should be as independent as possible. His father made a cane for Louis to swing in front of himself to keep from bumping into objects. The family included Louis in their chores, discussions, and outings. Soon, Louis learned to use the senses of smell, touch, and hearing to offset his lack of sight.

Still, Louis longed for everyday childhood experiences. Other children avoided him. They never understood how to throw bean bags or play hide-and-seek with a boy who was blind. Louis did have one special friend, Father Jacques Palluy. Father Palluy noticed how smart Louis was and invited him to the church for lessons a few mornings a week. Louis eagerly learned history, science, poetry , music, and Bible stories.

Louis's bright questions went beyond what Father Palluy could answer. The priest arranged for the six-year-old to attend the village school. Louis went to school with sighted children six days a week, from eight in the morning until five at night. He never tired from the long day as his class-mates did. Louis listened and remembered with remarkable ease. He figured math problems in his head faster than the other students did on paper. The only thing he could not do was read books.

By the time Louis turned ten, a new problem arose. Village children seldom attended school beyond their tenth birthday. The Brailles worried about what their blind son should do. Fortunately, Father Palluy suggested a plan. He learned of a Paris school for students who were blind. There, Louis could continue his lessons, and he could learn a trade. With Father Palluy's urging, Louis's parents agreed to let the boy go to Paris.

At first, Louis was terribly homesick. Everything was strange at school. He found himself in a large dormitory, sleeping, eating meals, and going to classes with so many boys he did not know. Gradually, however, Louis grew more comfortable at school. He also began making friends. Most important, Louis welcomed the chance to explore new subjects. The instructors quick-ly realized that their youngest student also was their brightest. For the first time, Louis learned to play musical instruments. He developed a remarkable talent on the piano and organ.

Another first was the opportunity to read. The school taught blind stu-dents to read books that were printed with raised letters. Students felt the enlarged letters with their fingertips. The idea was revolutionary at the time. But the system did not work very well. The letters had so many lines and curves that it took several seconds to feel a letter. And it took even longer to read an entire sentence. Also, the books were big and clumsy to handle. And they were so expensive to print that the Paris school owned only a few books. Louis read them all very quickly.

Louis knew there had to be a better way for people to read by touch. During the next few years, he worked constantly after class on a simpler sys-tem of creating books for the blind. He cut leather scraps into various forms that represented letters. He tried many methods, but they all had flaws.

One day, a French army captain named Charles Barbier visited the school. Captain Barbier had invented a system of sending messages in the dark called "night writing." Night writing used patterns of raised dots and dashes to represent parts of words. By feeling the patterns on the heavy paper, soldiers could decode messages in the dark. Louis thought that the system was perfect for short commands. The dot patterns were small enough that each character fit neatly under one's fingertip. The system needed improvements to provide an entire alphabet for the blind.

Louis spent the next three years refining Barbier's code. First, he created a six-dot pattern for each alphabet letter. Then he eliminated the dashes. At age fifteen, Louis had devised a writing system that became known as the "Braille system." It was a touchable alphabet that could make any writing accessible to the blind.

At first, educators rejected Louis's invention. They already had spent a considerable amount of money printing books containing their raised-letter system. But Louis's classmates loved his simple alphabet code. The Braille system opened the world of knowledge and literature to them. Their interest inspired Louis to create more symbols for mathematical signs and musical notes. Gradually , the Braille system gained popularity.

At seventeen, Louis became an instructor at the French National Institute for the Blind, where he remained until he died of tuberculosis at age forty-three. His fine organ playing earned him a position as church organist at one of the largest churches in Paris. But Louis's first passion remained books. Today, the Braille system is used worldwide, a tribute to the persistence of a young blind boy who wanted to read.

MARIA MITCHELL
ASTRONOMER AND MATHEMATICIAN
AT AGE TWELVE
1818–1889

Sea and sky meant everything to Nantucket islanders of the 1800s. Every man, woman, and child understood the importance of the stars in guiding ships safely. Young Maria Mitchell had a keen eye and questioning mind far beyond her years, and she dreamed of learning all that she could about the solar system.

Maria Mitchell seemed like any Quaker girl in Nantucket, a whaling port 30 miles (48 km) off the Massachusetts coast. As the third of ten children, Maria's days were filled with household chores and caring for younger brothers and sisters. She pumped water to wash dishes, peeled carrots and potatoes, and shelled peas from her father's farm.

There were few occasions for playtime in this serious Quaker community. Quakers believed in hard work above all else, and they frowned on idle play. Quaker children never went to carnivals, Christmas celebrations, or birthday parties. For fun, Maria and the other children collected flowers, shells, and fossil rocks.

Maria's greatest joy came at the end of the day, when she climbed to the roof of her house. Here, Maria and her father watched the stars. William Mitchell, an amateur astronomer, observed the stars so he could check the accuracy of chronometers (ships' clocks) for whaling captains. William pointed out the planets and stars, and his daughter measured the distances between them. As the moon moved across the sky, Maria wrote these nightly observations in her special notebook titled "Astronomy."

One day, Captain Bill Chadwick appeared at the house to have Maria's father check his chronometer. Lydia Mitchell was about to tell the captain that her husband was away from home. Just then, she felt a tug on her long skirt. Her daughter, Maria, begged to fix the captain's chronometer. She explained how she had learned to perform the task by watching her father work. Captain Chadwick had doubts about leaving his chronometer with a twelve-year-old. But no one else on the island could repair the instrument. He had little choice.

Anxiously, Maria waited for nightfall. The moment she saw stars in the sky, she began work on the chronometer with her father's sextant. The sextant measured the height of key stars. Maria compared that figure with the time on the chronometer. Then, she tested the time against the position of other stars. Maria repeated her observations again and again. When she was sure there were no mistakes, she went to bed. But Maria was so excited about the project that she awoke again that night to check the chronometer before morning. When Captain Chadwick arrived, he could not believe his eyes. The clever little girl had adjusted the chronometer perfectly.

Whenever she could get away from the other children, Maria studied mathematics and astronomy in a small closet at the foot of the stairs. The independent girl spent hours reading books and solving problems with her compasses and rulers. She had so many questions about the heavens. "Astronomy is not stargazing," she would say. "The entrance to astronomy is through mathematics." She thirsted to know more.

As Maria grew older, she studied with the Reverend Cyrus Pierce. Unlike her easygoing father, the minister required that "everything be wholly, precisely right." His demanding teaching, coupled with Quaker discipline, helped Maria develop her unusual ability to observe and calculate the wonders of the galaxy. "I was born of only ordinary capacity, but of extraordinary persistency," she later reflected.

By age seventeen, Maria had begun her own school. With a small advertisement in the paper, Maria attracted children to her one-room schoolhouse. Her pupils were rich and poor, white and African-American. The loving teacher taught her students as she had learned—by watching the world around her. Maria took her students to the rooftop and to the seashore, wherever there was something to learn. She wrote that she urged her students: "Learn to observe. The eye learns to see. Open yours wide to nature's revelations."

Meanwhile, Maria longed to continue her own studies. When she was offered a job as Nantucket librarian, she jumped at the chance to be around so many fine books. She read in the mornings and helped islanders in the library in the afternoons. Maria spent her evenings observing the stars.

One evening in 1847, Maria noticed a star she had never seen before. After checking and rechecking, her father announced that she had discovered a comet. It became known as the Maria Mitchell Comet.

News of the comet brought Maria fame and worldwide recognition as an astronomer. She received a gold medal from the king of Denmark and invitations to join many scientific organizations that were previously open only to men. Maria was the first woman to join the American Academy of Arts and Sciences and the American Association for the Advancement of Science.

In the 1860s, the founders of Vassar College were looking for a woman with Maria's reputation. Vassar was to be the first United States university for women, a college to rival the many traditional male-only schools. The college opened in 1865 with Maria on the staff as professor of astronomy. From the start, her simple, yet serious, teaching methods made her a favorite among students.

Maria became a tireless champion of equal rights for women and for women scientists. In 1873, she founded the Association for the Advancement of Women. At its meetings, Maria rallied for equal pay and recognition for women of all professions. The unending curiosity of a young girl eventually opened doors for many women who "opened their eyes to the universe around them."

JOHN EVERETT MILLAIS
GIFTED ARTIST AT AGE FOUR
1829–1896

Young John Everett Millais was constantly drawing. English seaside walks provided a wealth of interesting subjects—foamy waves, butterflies, birds, and many passersby also enjoying the scenery. After every walk, the boy remembered the people he met and drew their likenesses on paper.

John had a natural artistic talent that was nurtured by his mother. From the start, Mary Millais was John's strength and teacher. She provided much of his education in history, poetry, and literature. She saw to it that her son's interests were the focus of the family. When the Millais family moved to Brittany, in France, John became interested in medieval architecture. Mary prepared lessons about clothes and armor from the medieval period. For hours at a time, the six-year-old sketched swords, helmets, bows, and arrows for his book of armor.

For a brief time during his youth, John attended formal school. But he hated the restrictions of a daily grind. By the third day, the headmaster tried to whip John for disobeying. The insulted boy responded by biting the headmaster's hand. After John was expelled, he rejoiced at the prospect of being taught by his mother once again.

John's first formal art instruction came by accident. He and his older brother, William, were watching English soldiers marching to their nearby quarters. John studied an unusually large man dressed in bearskin with ornaments and a gold-topped cane. The burly man amused John so much that the boy took out his sketch pad and began to draw. To the boys' surprise, two soldiers watched them from behind. They especially liked John's drawing of their major.

The soldiers bought the picture from John, his first art sale. When the officers showed the picture to their fellow soldiers, none could believe that a six-year-old could draw so well. The officers brought John to the barracks and invited the men to bet on whether the lad could indeed draw. This time, John drew an even better likeness of the major. Winners of the bet received a free meal. And the officers went home with John to urge his parents to send him to art school.

The next year, John's family moved to St. Helier, where they had lived before his birth. There, the seven-year-old copied sculptures of heads under the direction of Mr. Bessel, the best art teacher the island had to offer. After a couple of years, Mr. Bessel announced that John had surpassed what he could teach him. The family would have to move to London and seek better training.

Once in London, John eagerly sketched classic paintings in the British Museum while waiting for a school vacancy. Unlike other city boys who played football, John and William loved to play "National Gallery." The boys knew all the paintings in this famous London art museum. Their game involved re-creating these masterpieces at home for visitors to see.

At age nine, John amazed the audience at a Society of Arts competition, where he went to school. The small boy stood on a stool to receive his silver medal. His historical painting, *The Battle of Bannockburn*, triumphed over art from candidates as old as thirty.

The following year, John became the youngest student to attend the esteemed Royal Academy Schools. During the next six years, he earned every honor the Society of Arts awarded. By the time he was seventeen years old, John's paintings were attracting attention across Europe. French critics claimed his *Pizarro Seizing the Inca of Peru* was the greatest historical art of the year.

As his work gained recognition, John grew more dissatisfied with the stiff styles practiced by most artists. Raphael, an early sixteenth-century artist, was worshiped in the art world. But John saw Raphael as the reason artists lacked creativity and realism in their work.

To free art from stifling custom, John and another artist formed the Pre-Raphaelite Brotherhood. As an adult, John influenced the art world as an educator and as president of the Royal Academy. He painted portraits and popular subjects. But he always kept the same interest and technical skill he developed as a natural-born young artist.

CHILD LABOR IN THE UNITED STATES

Until the eighteenth century, children took part in the same work as their parents. Farm children woke at dawn and labored until sundown. In growing towns, children helped at home with work that their parents received from bosses. They assembled products or sewed garments, and the family earned money for each piece that was completed. By the end of the 1700s, this manufacturing work was beginning to be done in large factories that were being built.

In Great Britain in the late 1700s, machines were invented for spinning and weaving yarn. With these machines, factories could produce massive quantities of cloth. The change to producing goods in factories became known as the Industrial Revolution. In the 1800s, businesses in large cities depended upon factories that employed hundreds of workers. Because of improved machines, fewer workers produced better cloth faster, and at lower cost.

Many mill owners saw another benefit—machines that were simple to run. Some machines were easy enough for a child to operate. Therefore, many mill owners hired children, who received lower wages than adults. Owners said that these children would be better off in a factory than on the streets. In truth, however, factory labor exposed children to many new dangers.

Child labor was common in Great Britain by the time mills appeared in America. In 1789, the first American cotton mill was built in Rhode Island by an Englishman named Samuel Slater. Slater imported the practice of employing children. He opened the mill with nine children who ran his spinning machines. Within ten years, he employed more than one hundred children between the ages of four and ten. At the same time, other mills were established in North America, and many also employed children.

Mill children had hard lives. Days were long, and factory conditions were awful. Most boys and girls awoke at 5:00 A.M. to the piercing sound of a mill whistle. They quickly washed, dressed in tattered clothes, and ran through cold, dark streets to the factory. At 6:00 A.M., the whistle blared again. Mill doors shut. Anyone who was late by even one minute lost an hour of pay. Sometimes latecomers were fired.

Young children worked a variety of jobs at the mill. Bobbin boys watched thread feed from huge spools, or bobbins, onto the looms that wove cloth. If a thread broke, the youngsters tied the ends together. They also replaced empty bobbins with full ones. Each boy guarded a row of machines. Climbing on machines to change bobbins was hazardous work. Frequently, bobbin boys took off their shoes so they could climb more easily. But if a child slipped, he fell to the floor. Sometimes, a child fell into the moving parts of the machine. A slip could mean serious injury, or even death.

Every mill job was a danger to child workers. Girls who greased machines risked being snared by a whirling wheel, which could pull clumps of hair, or even a piece of scalp, from a head. Exhausted children forced themselves to stay alert for fear of losing a body part to the machines. Mill children suffered from terrible headaches because the roar of the machines was loud and constant. They developed aches and pains from standing or sitting in the same position all day. Overall, conditions in the mill were filthy, dark, cold, noisy, and dangerous.

Mill children toiled this way twelve hours a day, six days a week. The only breaks were fifteen minutes for breakfast and thirty minutes for lunch. By the end of the day, children went home and fell into bed, too tired to eat the food their meager wages bought.

Parents accepted child labor because they had little choice. In the United States, New England farmers were finding it difficult to farm the region's stony, infertile soil. Men went to work at the mills that were sprouting up along New England streams and rivers.

Initially, women and children stayed home to tend the farms. As manufacturers built more mills, families moved closer to the towns that grew near the mills. Bosses began firing the men and hiring women and children to get more workers for less pay. Unable to find work, grown men lived off their children's wages. Younger and younger children went to work to maintain the family. The cycle of poverty was so strong that individual parents were powerless to protect their children.

Children became a larger share of the workforce as the Industrial Revolution expanded to many eastern U.S. cities in the 1800s. Increasingly, factory owners discovered the advantages of hiring cheap and useful child labor. Thousands of youngsters tended coal chutes in mines; removed glass bottles from hot furnaces in glassworks; filled and sealed sharp metal cans in canneries; operated rotating saws in lumber mills; and sewed clothing in textile factories. By 1832, 40 percent of the workers hired for New England textile mills were between the ages of seven and sixteen.

In cities, children slaved in a variety of jobs outside the factory. Some sold newspapers or became food vendors. Others delivered packages, took care of stabled horses, or set pins in bowling alleys.

Long hours and unhealthy work conditions exposed young workers to a high rate of accidents and diseases. Doctors and newspapers reported the cruel treatment that these "wage slaves" suffered. Teachers claimed that, without opportunity to acquire an education or to learn a trade, these children were doomed to the same awful lives as their parents—if they lived that long.

Gradually, groups of concerned adults organized to oppose child labor. Wealthy social reformers and clergy raised their voices against poor working conditions. Authors such as Charles Dickens detailed the sad lives of working street children. In America, Sarah N. Cleghorn wrote this poem after watching men play golf outside a southern cotton mill:

> *The golf links lie so near the mill*
> *That almost every day*
> *The laboring children can look out*
> *And see the men at play.*

The verse mocks the sad truth that grown men played, while children performed adult work within each other's sight.

Large-scale reform was slow to take hold. In 1802, Great Britain was the first country to pass a law restricting child labor, and Germany followed in 1833. In the United States, newly formed organizations appealed to lawmakers to end child labor abuse and to establish required school attendance. Worker groups such as the Knights of Labor were formed to fight their own battles, including efforts to introduce bills to regulate child labor.

Massachusetts enacted the first state child labor law in the United States in 1836. Under this law, children under fifteen could work in factories only if they had already attended three months of school. A few states followed with limited rulings prohibiting factory owners from hiring children under ten or twelve years of age. The laws were a small beginning. Like those in Britain, these laws were passed without means of enforcement. Too many poor families needed their children to work, and the government seemed unwilling to challenge big business.

One of the strongest organizations to oppose child labor was the National Child Labor Committee. This group united key leaders from twenty-two states and many different industries with growing worker organizations. The committee's goal was to draw national attention to the evils of child labor. To educate the public, the group sent investigators to mines, farms, and factories to observe treatment of children on the job. Representatives took pictures and wrote reports that they published in a quarterly bulletin. For years, the National Child Labor Committee met regularly and pressed lawmakers for reform.

In 1916, Congress passed the first federal child labor law. The law established minimum ages for certain types of work; set an eight-hour workday six days a week; and prohibited night work for children under age sixteen. The National Child Labor Committee saw the legislation as a breakthrough, but their hopes were dashed within two years. After pressure from the manufacturers, the Supreme Court declared the law unconstitutional.

There were many halfhearted attempts at state and national reform. By the early 1930s, only 50 percent of the states had any child labor laws, and these laws were usually weak. The first federal law to uphold child labor reform successfully came in 1938. The Fair Labor Standards Act established the minimum age for working children at sixteen years for most jobs. If the U.S. secretary of labor deemed a profession too dangerous for children, nobody under eighteen could perform those jobs. Fourteen- and fifteen-year-olds could work a limited number of hours during nonschool hours. All children were required to attend school until they were sixteen.

The Fair Labor Standards Act was the only child labor reform law to be upheld by the Supreme Court and backed by federal and local governments. Although the fight for basic children's rights continued, government supplied the framework for real reform. But it was the children who labored under horrible conditions for more than a century who made the law necessary. Their contribution to history always will be remembered.

IDA LEWIS
RESCUER AND LIGHTHOUSE KEEPER
AT AGE FOURTEEN
1842–1911

Lighthouse keepers were very important to nineteenth-century New England coastal towns. Harbor lights repeatedly had to be cleaned and relit with whale oil. Otherwise, boats might crash against the rocky coast at night or in sudden storms.

When Ida Lewis was twelve years old, her father was appointed keeper of the Lime Rock Lighthouse in Newport, Rhode Island. Ida was the oldest daughter of Hosea and Idawalley Lewis's four children. Before the lighthouse job, Ida spent her days in school or helping at home, much like other children in Newport. But life changed when the Lewis family moved into a house next to the lighthouse. Thereafter, everything centered around keeping the light burning.

Ida followed her father everywhere in the lighthouse. She learned that a lighthouse keeper's job required constant care and devotion. The lighthouse needed to be kept in tip-top shape at all times. During the day, Ida helped her father scrub and paint the lighthouse. Their legs ached from hours of trudging up and down the steep spiral staircase to the tower. Sometimes, they stayed up all night cleaning and tending to the lamp during storms. After heavy storms, the lighthouse needed many repairs.

In 1857, tragedy struck the Lewis family. Ida's father became too ill to work. Now, the entire burden of the lighthouse fell on young Ida. Moreover, Ida rowed her sister and brothers to and from Newport, where they attended school and shopped for supplies.

One day, Ida's mother noticed storm clouds forming. She called her elder daughter to bring the younger children from school before the northwest wind stirred the winds too high. Ida ran outside, saw the clouds, and bolted toward the fishing boat.

She rowed as quickly as she could against the swelling waves. Ida knew she must return to the lighthouse quickly. The harbor provided the only light to passing ships in a storm. And she had to maintain the lighthouse in the storm.

After picking up the children and returning across a choppy harbor, Ida delivered her frightened siblings safe at home. Everyone ran to the comfort of their mother—except Ida. She ran through a downpour for the lighthouse. She climbed the slippery steps to the tower. Just as she reached the top, she saw the last flicker of light from the lamp.

Ida searched quickly for a jar of whale oil and added it to the lamp. Then she wiped the outside of the lamp so the light shone brighter. After the light was safely in place, she shook out of her dripping clothes and rested. The storm raged all night, and Ida rode it out, alone atop the lighthouse. She forced herself to stay awake all night, for she knew only she could provide light for ships in the storm at sea. When the terrible storm ended, news of her bravery reached the mainland. She became the unofficial lighthouse keeper of Lime Rock.

As lighthouse keeper, Ida had many occasions to save lives. When Ida was barely fifteen, she noticed four young men in the water. Their boat had overturned in rough waves offshore. When she heard their desperate screams, Ida realized that none of the foolhardy boys knew how to swim. At once, Ida ran to her boat and rowed toward the thrashing boys. The fearless girl rowed through the choppy water and reached the young men just as their strength gave out. She pulled the boys into the boat one at a time. Then she rowed them to safety.

Two years later, Ida rowed into Newport Harbor and rescued two drowning sailors whose boat had capsized. She resuscitated them from unconsciousness after dragging them ashore. A year after that, Ida again acted heroically. Three herders waded too far out in the harbor to retrieve a lost sheep. Ida pulled the men to safety, and then she returned to the water to drag the animal ashore. Ida saved several more drowning people during her teenage years.

Newspapers reported Ida's heroic adventures. Honors and letters of praise poured in from across the nation. The governor of Rhode Island presented Ida with a medal. President Ulysses S. Grant visited Lime Rock just to meet the girl who had saved so many lives.

Ida remained at the lighthouse until her death at age sixty-nine. By then, she had rescued about twenty people during her fifty-four-year career as lighthouse keeper.

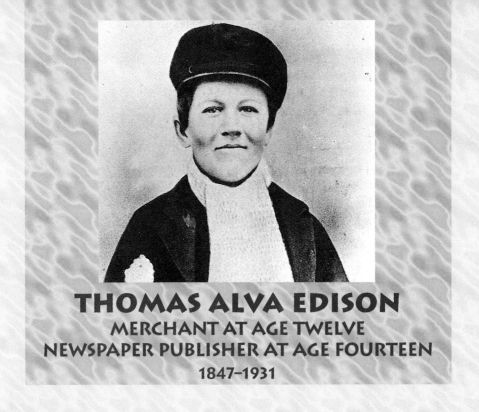

THOMAS ALVA EDISON
MERCHANT AT AGE TWELVE
NEWSPAPER PUBLISHER AT AGE FOURTEEN
1847–1931

Thomas Alva Edison was always a curious child. His parents said he asked more questions than their three older children put together. His parents were concerned by the ways that Thomas (or Alva, as they called him) put newly found information into use. He explored his world with an intense desire to discover. Once he sat on a nest of goose eggs to get them to hatch. Another time he set the barn on fire just to observe what the flames would do. A public flogging from his father did little to dampen his enthusiasm for experiments.

Alva's thirst for knowledge made him a difficult student for strict teachers. His constant questions were out of step with the education of the eighteenth century. Children were to speak only when spoken to. They were whipped if they talked out of turn. Instead of memorizing facts and rules, Alva fidgeted and daydreamed. The teacher thought he was slow-witted. After Alva went to school for only three months, his mother decided to teach her boy at home.

Alva blossomed under his mother's guidance. Nancy Edison bought an interesting assortment of books to challenge her son. Together they read advanced history books and classic works by William Shakespeare and Charles Dickens. By his ninth birthday, Alva had read books that many adults could not understand.

The most exciting book Alva read was R. G. Parker's *School of Natural Philosophy*, a basic science text. After devouring this text, the boy begged his parents for more science books. When he learned all he could from books, Alva assembled a science lab to test Parker's experiments. He even built a simple telegraph. At the time, this was the most recent invention for sending messages by wire over long distances.

The more Alva read, the more he wanted to experiment. He decided to get a job as newsboy with the new Grand Trunk Railroad, which extended between Port Huron, Michigan, where the Edisons lived, and Detroit. He planned to give most of his earnings to his mother. The rest would help pay for chemicals and supplies for his experiments.

At twelve years of age, Alva began working for about a dollar a day as one of the youngest railroad newsboys. He sold newspapers, candy, and sandwiches from 7:00 A.M. until 9:30 P.M. With such long hours, Alva thought he should be making more money. The conductor gave him permission to run a store from the baggage car. Alva supplied the store with groceries he bought from local markets along the train route. The business was so successful that Alva hired two helpers. After paying his employees, Thomas still made twenty dollars a week.

When the Civil War broke out, people wanted news from battlefronts. Alva ended his grocery business and focused on newspaper sales. He discovered that if telegraph operators sent newspaper headlines ahead to railroad stops, news-hungry customers met the train and bought his newspapers. Alva's business soared. His sales rose from one hundred papers a day to one thousand!

Between station stops, Alva found plenty of time for his favorite occupation—chemistry experiments. The conductor allowed him to use part of the baggage car for his laboratory. Because newspaper sales were so big, Alva decided he should start his own newspaper in the laboratory. At age fourteen, he bought a second-hand press and became reporter, printer, publisher, and distributor of the *Grand Trunk Herald*, the first newspaper ever published on a moving train. Soon Alva had four hundred happy customers reading the latest news from up and down the railroad line.

Alva's railroad career ended suddenly after one of his chemicals caught fire on the baggage-car floor. The conductor helped both Alva and his laboratory to a hasty exit at the next station. Alva moved his experiments back home to Port Huron. Now he had time to pursue another interest—the telegraph.

An accident helped Alva make his dream of becoming a telegraph operator come true. As he was standing in a railroad station, Alva noticed a boxcar rolling toward the station agent's son. He called to the boy, but the youngster continued playing on the track. Just as the boxcar was almost upon the child, Alva lunged at him and rolled both of them to safety. The grateful station agent offered to repay Alva by teaching him to operate the telegraph and giving him a job as assistant train dispatcher.

Alva saw the telegraph as more than providing a job. It was equipment to explore and improve. When Alva was sixteen, he attached an alarm clock to the telegraph so it would send messages at specific times. Alva's bosses rejected the idea, thinking it was a way for a lazy boy to avoid sending messages.

But Thomas Edison continued to create new inventions. Many were highly successful. He received his first patent for an electric vote-counting machine. As an adult, Edison invented the light bulb, phonograph, motion-picture camera, microphone, waxed paper, and gas mask. His improvements on the telegraph and telephone opened communication around the world.

At the time of his death at the age of eighty-four, Thomas Alva Edison had been granted 1,093 U.S. patents—more than any other American. Many of his inventions paved the way for the electronics age of the late twentieth century. The little boy with the curious mind grew up to change the course of civilization.

CHARLES MILLER
PONY EXPRESS RIDER AT AGE ELEVEN
1850–1955

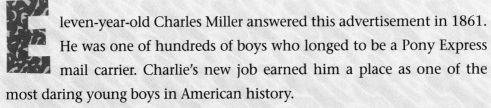

WANTED

Young Skinny Wiry Fellows, not over eighteen.
Must be expert riders willing to risk death daily.
Orphans preferred. Wages $25 per week.

leven-year-old Charles Miller answered this advertisement in 1861. He was one of hundreds of boys who longed to be a Pony Express mail carrier. Charlie's new job earned him a place as one of the most daring young boys in American history.

Charlie came from a pioneer family. He was born in a covered wagon traveling west in the mid-1800s. Like countless others, the Millers headed west to search for land. They hoped to build a new life in a place they thought was full of adventure. To thousands of Easterners, the West was an untouched landscape, open for the taking. Charlie's family settled in northern California. His father dug their first home out of the base of Mount Shasta in Modoc County. They made a clearing to grow vegetables and grain for the oxen. Wild berries, animals, and trout from the stream provided all the food they needed.

Charlie Miller's early life was filled with little playtime. All day, he worked the family ranch. Often, he went with his father to gather stray wild horses that roamed across their fields. Charlie's job was to "break," or train, the wild horses to be ridden and to perform labor.

At the time, countless other ranchers, farmers, railroad workers, and miners established new towns and cities throughout the North American West. Every town opened general stores to supply settlers with food, tools, and other goods. But one precious supply the settlers also wanted was news from back east.

Telegraph lines and railroads ran from New York City to as far west as St. Joseph, Missouri. From Missouri to the West Coast, the fastest method of carrying news was by stagecoach. Stagecoaches traveled winding, rocky routes and had many stops, so they took more than three weeks to deliver mail to California.

A Missouri businessman, William Russell, decided to open a private mail service. Russell mapped out a straight route to be traversed by riders who would frequently change horses. The route would take only ten days. Russell's company built 190 stations 10 to 15 miles (16 to 24 km) apart along 1,800 miles (2,880 km) of unsettled wilderness. He then bought four hundred horses and placed newspaper ads for pony riders.

On April 3, 1860, the first Pony Express riders set off. One rider headed west from St. Joseph, Missouri, and another rode east from Sacramento, California. Each carried saddlebags filled with mail. At relay stations, they mounted fresh horses and continued riding. At the end of the day, they transferred their mailbags to riders who carried the mail on the next leg of the journey.

Twelve-year-old Charlie Miller saw one of Russell's ads on a supply trip into town. The thought of forging new trails and carrying important mail lit a fire in the boy. Charlie applied for the job and was soon accepted. The Pony Express needed young, light men and even boys because heavier riders would tire the horses. About eighty teenagers became Pony Express riders. Charlie Miller was the youngest.

Charlie's route took him from Carson City, Nevada, to Sacramento, California. The trail was dangerous for a boy or an adult. American Indians lived in the hills along Charlie's route. The Indians were native to the territory, and they feared that the Pony Express would bring more settlers to their land. Most of the time, Charlie outran the Indians, but some attacks left him with scars from arrow wounds.

In addition to encounters with unfriendly Indians, Pony Express riders faced challenges from nature. They rode across blazing hot deserts and through frigid blizzards. Because the hazards were so great, riders were paid well. Most earned between $100 and $150 a month.

The riders were dedicated to their jobs. Many competed for faster riding times. The fastest ride was made to deliver a copy of President Abraham Lincoln's first address to Congress. The document was carried from Missouri to California in seven days, seventeen hours. In its brief life, the Pony Express successfully delivered more than 30,000 pieces of mail and lost only one bag of mail.

The Pony Express lasted only eighteen months. New technology led to the company's early ruin. The first message by transcontinental telegraph was sent on October 24, 1861. With an electronic link between the two coasts, William Russell knew his mail route was doomed. Just two days later, Russell closed the Pony Express.

Charlie Miller moved on to seek new thrills. For a while, he was a ranch hand and broncobuster in California. From there, he went south and patrolled the U.S.-Mexico border as a Texas Ranger. He also broke horses for

Theodore Roosevelt, who later became president of the United States. Still seeking adventure, Charlie joined Buffalo Bill's Wild West Show and fought in World War I.

By 1931, automobiles had replaced horses, but Charlie decided to make one last mail run by horse across the country. At the age of eighty-one, Charlie left New Jersey and rode 30 miles (48 km) a day until he reached California. He was the only person ever to complete the trip on horseback. The journey took seven months and twenty-three days through snow, rain, and sandstorm. By then, this hero of the Old West was called "Bronco Charlie." He lived to the age of 105. He was the longest-lived Pony Express rider and one of the last legendary pioneers.

DRUMMER BOYS

William Howe gave each of his two sons a drum and taught them to play. At first, neighbors cringed at the sounds they made. But with practice, the boys became good enough to earn money playing for Sunday school picnics and other public functions. These early performances served as training for a much bigger job—as drummer boys for the army during the Civil War (1861–65).

Drummer boys played a small but significant role in America's earliest battles. They assisted troops in many wars, beginning with the Revolutionary War (1775–83) and continuing throughout the early 1800s. These young soldiers guided regiments through battle with little more than a drum and pair of sticks.

Drummers served as the main communication links between military troops and officers. (The telegraph, first invented in 1844, was not widely available until the 1860s.) Drumbeats of differing patterns summoned units to arms and communicated battle plans. Without drummer boys, messages would have taken much longer to reach troops spread across acres and miles.

Drummer boys provided uplifting rhythms to inspire weary marching troops. When they were not playing instruments, drummer boys helped wherever needed. In camp, they carried water to soldiers. After battle, they braved the grim tasks of removing the wounded, sharpening surgical instruments, and burying the dead.

Drummer communications were so necessary to the war effort that early armies provided special uniforms for the boys. Drummers wore opposite colors of those worn by regular soldiers. That way, officers easily spotted the young musicians when their services were needed.

Another benefit of wearing different uniforms was the ability to stand out in battle. Frequently, drummers led their battalions onto battlefields. An unwritten code prohibited enemy armies from attacking the unarmed youths. Their uniforms warned the distant enemy that these soldiers were without protection. Still, many boys died in the flurry of crossfire.

Most drummers were between twelve and sixteen years of age. Lyston Howe became a drummer boy when he was only ten. He was so short that his adult-size drum dragged on the ground, even with the straps shortened to the last hole. The thrill of soldiering was so great that after a bout with the measles, he immediately reenlisted in the army.

Orion, Lyston's younger brother, was away at school when the Civil War began. By the summer of 1862, war fever hit the fourteen-year-old, and he left school to join his brother and father, who were serving in the same army unit. The three Howes served together for a short time before William retired for health reasons.

The two boys became 55th Infantry mascots. According to army documents: Our infant drummers attracted much attention on dressed parade or at great camps of instruction at Camp Douglas, even rivaling our original giant color guard. They were both small for their years. The little Howes drummed well, proved hardy, never seemed homesick, were treated as regimental pets, and passed through battle after battle and march after march, untouched by disease, unscathed by bullet and shell.

Both boys saw extensive battle and received recognition. Orion earned the Medal of Honor, the nation's highest military award, for his bravery at the Battle of Vicksburg. A sergeant at Vicksburg instructed Orion that fighting troops must have a constant supply of cartridges to win the battle. Orion collected unused gun cartridges from dead and wounded soldiers and took them to the front. He bravely crossed a ravine several times, dodging bullets along the way. During one storm of musketballs, witnesses saw the boy fall wounded. But Orion managed to continue his journey and deliver a message to General Sherman requesting more cartridges. General Sherman wrote later:

> What renews my memory of the fact now is, that one so young, carrying a musket-ball wound through his leg, should have found his way to me on that fatal spot, and delivered his message, not forgetting the very important part, even of the caliber of the musket, 54, which you know is an unusual one.

At the end of his letter, General Sherman recommended that Orion be admitted to the Naval Academy. President Abraham Lincoln made the appointment himself, a year later, when Orion's wounds healed. Orion continued to fight, until he was wounded again before entering the Naval Academy. He saw more action in battle before retiring from the military and becoming a dentist in Sutton, Nebraska.

Lyston Howard served more than six years as drummer boy, the longest career of any young Civil War drummer. He was wounded in battle and marched with adult soldiers who were hungry and sick. Upon discharge, Lyston came home to Illinois, where he became a successful businessman who pioneered factory equipment to wash coal.

The end of the Civil War signaled the end of child foot soldiers. In March 1864, Congress voted to limit military recruitment to males over age sixteen. Drumming was replaced by bugles and telegraphs, which provided more efficient ways to transmit messages among fighting units. Still, the memory of patriotic youths such as Lyston and Orion Howe remains a vital part of American history.

JOHN PHILIP SOUSA
UNITED STATES MARINE CORPS BAND
MEMBER AT AGE THIRTEEN
1854–1932

Tramp, tramp, tramp . . . the boys are marching! Eleven-year-old John Philip Sousa could not get the tune to this song out of his head. He and his father, Antonio, had just come from a parade of triumphant Union Army soldiers. The Civil War had ended recently, and thousands of people lined Pennsylvania Avenue in Washington, D.C., to cheer the ragged, but joyful, returning regiments.

John was proud of his father, a trombonist in the United States Marine Corps Band. John spent hours listening to the band practice, but he thought the songs they played sounded odd. The music seemed out of step with the victorious occasion and the excited crowds honoring the soldiers. Maybe that was because the marching music was written by composers from another time and other lands. John decided to compose and play new marches, songs that honored American pride.

John was always a determined child. At five he decided to punish his mother for not allowing him to eat a donut. He ran outdoors and hid in the yard. He did not respond to his mother's worried calls, even after a rainstorm erupted. When Mrs. Sousa finally found him, he was soaked and shivering. John's prank resulted in a dangerous case of pneumonia. The illness sapped his strength for nearly two years.

John continued to get into scrapes because of his bold actions. But his mischief often was overlooked because he was a good student and a talented young musician. Members of his father's band said young John had natural talent. As a young boy, he learned to play the flute, cornet, trombone, French horn, and violin. He developed the ability to "sight-read" music. This meant that he could look at printed music and play the song immediately, without any study. John also could repeat a melody after hearing it played a single time.

When John was eleven, he organized a band of seven musicians. Then he booked the band to play at Professor Sheldon's Fashionable Dance Academy on Saturdays. John appointed himself first violinist and leader of the band, which included mostly adults. After a few performances, the men tricked John. They told him to demand more money from the professor, or they would quit. The professor refused, and John quit the job. But the band continued to play on Saturdays—with a new leader.

John was disappointed about the band, but he grew more determined to improve his musical skills. Ever since he saw the victory parade in Washington, John had been eager to compose and play marching songs. He read whatever he could find about composition and practiced violin for hours.

One hot day when thirteen-year-old John was practicing with the parlor window open, a stranger knocked at the door. The nicely dressed caller introduced himself as bandleader of the traveling circus that was in town. He liked John's playing so much that he invited the boy to join the circus for twelve dollars a week. The only problem was that he would have to leave his family when the circus left town that week.

John could hardly believe his ears. Here was his chance to earn money as a musician without years of schooling. At the same time, he was happy living with his family and did not want to leave home. The choice was difficult, but he decided to sneak away without asking for his parents' permission.

Meanwhile, Antonio Sousa learned about his son's plan, and he worked on a scheme of his own. The next day before John could leave, Antonio grabbed his son and marched him to the Marine Commandant's headquarters. Antonio had arranged for his son to be admitted into the United States Marine Corps Band, the youngest musician to receive the honor.

At first, John assumed the duties of an apprentice. He ran errands, arranged sheet music, and shined brass buckles on uniforms. As his violin and trombone playing improved, John played with the band when other musicians were absent. He also was allowed to perform in concerts with other bands and to tutor music students privately.

Despite his busy schedule, John pursued his dream of writing march music. At fifteen, he completed his first composition. It was another three years before he published two more songs. Slowly, John's composing and playing talents were becoming known to theater and dance orchestras.

Seven years after John enlisted, he left the Marine Corps Band to establish himself as a conductor and composer. However, his musical talents became so highly regarded that the Marine Corps recalled him to rebuild the band's sagging reputation. Under John's direction, the Marine Corps Band reached national renown. Then John formed his own band. This group extended John's fame in the United States and in Europe.

John Philip Sousa's greatest accomplishments were his many compositions. His lively, patriotic marches, such as "Stars and Stripes Forever" and "The Washington Post," were wildly popular. They quickly became identified as truly American music. Nearly a century after he lived, a "Sousa march" continues to stir patriotic spirit.

CECILIA ROSE O'NEILL
PUBLISHED CARTOONIST AT AGE FOURTEEN
1874–1944

ecilia Rose O'Neill was a creative, yet unruly, child. Cecilia came from an educated family that constantly weathered hard times. Her father's frequent job changes kept the family on the move. Cecilia was born in Wilkes-Barre, Pennsylvania, and as a child, she lived in many homes before her family settled in Omaha, Nebraska. Continual change only added to the household disorder and Cecilia's untamed ways.

In school, Cecilia became known for being odd. She recited love poems with the emotion of an adult. She sewed her own clothes, which were very different from the styles of the day. In everything she did, Cecilia sought to please herself, no matter how much attention she attracted.

Cecilia was a dreamer. She treasured long walks in the woods to experience nature. Many days, Cecilia and her father took strolls together. Wherever they stopped, they read and discussed poetry, Shakespeare, or Greek mythology. Cecilia brought her sketchbook on these walks to capture the beauty around her on paper. During one of these outings, Cecilia is said to have announced her plan to paint and write. "I see my future in the blue Nebraska sky," she said.

Cecilia developed an interest in all the arts at an early age. She spent much of her time in the library, eagerly reading about art history and modern drawing. However, Cecilia never copied pictures from the masters, as young artists often do. Nor did she receive formal art lessons.

In 1888, Cecilia had the opportunity to keep the promise she made to her father. The Omaha *World Herald* offered a prize for the student with the best art drawing. Cecilia drew a picture of a woman with flowing robes from classical mythology and called it *Temptation*. The sketch was too good— the judges refused to believe the girl had drawn it. After proving her talent to them, Cecilia received the prize. She won the opportunity to illustrate a weekly cartoon series for the newspaper.

Within a year, Cecilia was earning a good salary and pursuing a double career in art and writing. The years of walks and library study had led to writing serious poetry and the beginnings of a novel.

At nineteen, Cecilia left home for New York. She longed to publish her novel and illustrate magazine stories. Her training at the Omaha *World Herald* opened many doors. By Cecilia's twentieth birthday, leading magazines from the United States and England were bidding against each other for her artwork.

Cecilia's drawings soon appeared in *Life*, *Ladies' Home Journal*, *Good Housekeeping*, and other popular magazines of the day. She signed these early works only with her initials. Magazine illustration was considered "man's work" at the turn of the century.

As an adult, Cecilia was best known for her drawings of elf-like "Kewpies." At first, Kewpies adorned poems or stories in *Ladies' Home Journal*. Then the warm-hearted creatures became part of Cecilia's cartoon strips in which they performed good deeds. Cecilia recalled that these fanciful cupids were inspired by her baby brother, whom she had cared for as a child. Kewpies touched so many readers that manufacturers reproduced them as cutouts and dolls. Kewpies became a big business.

The unusual young girl with a wonderful imagination grew into a self-made woman who was a skilled illustrator, poet, author, sculptor, and creator of the famous Kewpies.

HELEN KELLER
TRIUMPHED OVER SENSORY DISABILITIES
AT AGE TEN
1880–1968

At birth, Helen Keller was healthy and normal. But when she was nineteen months old, a serious illness left her both blind and deaf. During the months that followed, Helen explored her silent, dark world with her hands. The youngster developed a system of signals to let her parents and two older stepbrothers know what she wanted.

By age five, Helen understood much of what went on around her. She also knew that she lacked the ability to communicate with her mouth the way her family did. Helen became so upset at trying to make herself understood that she frequently threw tantrums. She became so uncontrollable that her parents decided to hire a teacher to help them train her.

The Kellers traveled to many doctors before they could locate a teacher for Helen. Finally, Dr. Alexander Graham Bell, the same man who invented the telephone, gave them the address of the Perkins Institute for the Blind in Boston. Mr. Keller contacted the institute and arranged for a teacher to come to the family's home in Tuscumbia, Alabama.

Helen later wrote in her autobiography, *The Story of My Life*, that the most important day of her life was March 3, 1887. That was the day when her teacher, Anne Sullivan, arrived. "I was caught up and held close in the arms of her who had come to reveal all things to me, and, more than all things else, to love me," Helen wrote.

Anne Sullivan's first job was to tame her unruly student. The stubborn girl refused to cooperate with her teacher. Sullivan moved into a cottage on the grounds with Helen so that they could work together without the rest of the family disturbing their lessons. Helen soon discovered that her angry outbursts did not affect her teacher the way they did her family.

Anne Sullivan proved a firm, but loving, teacher. From the beginning, she talked to Helen as she would to any other child. She communicated by tracing letters and words with her fingers in the palm of Helen's hand. For example, Sullivan spelled d-o-l-l, gave Helen a doll, and had Helen imitate the finger spelling. Helen caught on to the finger spelling quickly. But she had trouble with the idea that things like dolls had names.

After many weeks of work, Anne Sullivan was trying to help Helen understand the difference between a mug and water. As they walked past a water pump, Sullivan thrust Helen's hand under the spout. Something about the water running down her hand connected with a word that Helen had learned before her illness. Suddenly, the meaning of water, and of all language, became clear. Helen later wrote, "That living word [water] awakened my soul, gave it light, hope, joy, set it free!"

From then on, Helen wanted to know the names of everything. She learned about the ideas and feelings that words expressed. "As my knowledge grew I felt more and more the delight of the world I was in," recorded Helen.

By the time Helen was eight, Anne Sullivan knew that Helen understood enough words to begin reading words printed in raised letters. Sullivan took Helen to the Perkins Institute to continue her education. Helen was delighted to fingerspell with other children like herself and to read books written in Braille, a coded system of letters with small raised dots. For the next few years, Helen explored arithmetic, literature, German, and French.

During that time, Helen decided that she wanted to speak like hearing children. Anne Sullivan introduced her to Sarah Fuller, principal of Boston's Horace Mann School for the Deaf. Fuller agreed to give Helen speech lessons. She let Helen feel how her lips and tongue formed sounds. After only eleven lessons, Helen spoke in a halting, but understandable, manner.

— *Helen Keller (left) "hears" Anne Sullivan by feeling vibrations on her lips.* —

By the age of ten, Helen was becoming famous. Newspapers and magazines reported the remarkable story of how quickly Helen had gained so many skills. Still, Helen had one more mountain she wanted to climb. The girl who loved to learn wanted to graduate from college.

In 1894, Helen enrolled in schools that would improve her speech and give her the coursework to apply to college. In 1900, Helen entered Radcliffe College with Anne Sullivan by her side to translate lessons. Four years later, Helen graduated with honors. While at Radcliffe, Helen wrote her autobiography. The story told of her struggle to learn. Many years later, Helen Keller's *The Story of My Life* inspires people with and without disabilities.

As an adult, Helen devoted her life to helping individuals who were poor or disabled. One of her greatest accomplishments was an improvement to the Braille reading system. In addition, she wrote articles and books and traveled around the world making speeches to raise money for these causes. By the time she died at age eighty-eight, Helen was known and admired by millions. She remains one of the greatest heroes of our time.

RACHEL CARSON
PUBLISHED AUTHOR AT AGE ELEVEN
1907–1964

Rachel Carson's father could have been a rich man. The Carsons' family farm was located near Pittsburgh, Pennsylvania, a region where coal deposits lie underground. But Mr. Carson refused to sell his farm whenever a big mining company tried to buy his farm. Land was all the wealth the Carsons needed.

As a young girl, Rachel Carson learned from her mother to appreciate the outdoors. Mrs. Carson took her daughter on long walks to explore wildlife in the woods and streams near their home. Often, the two awoke before dawn to hear the birds' first morning calls.

As soon as Rachel could read, her mother fed her a steady diet of books on science. At night, the family gathered around the piano to sing songs and read poems and stories. Rachel's favorites were about nature, especially the sea. After these sessions, Rachel went to bed dreaming of the ocean, which she never had seen.

Rachel decided at an early age to become a writer. The young girl understood that someone had to write all the wonderful science books she enjoyed. But she also wanted to create fictional stories.

When Rachel was ten, she decided to write a story for the children's magazine *St. Nicholas*. In every issue, the magazine published stories written by talented children and teenagers. An idea for a story came to Rachel in a letter from her older brother, Robert. He was away from home, a soldier in World War I. In his letter, Robert told a story about a brave pilot he had met who had continued flying after a wing was shot off his plane.

Rachel wrote out her own version of the story. Then she spent many hours revising it. She changed words and rearranged sentences. Later, Rachel said that "writing was largely a matter of . . . hard work, of writing and rewriting endlessly until you are satisfied that you have said what you want to say as clearly and simply as possible." When she felt the story was finished, Rachel showed it to her mother. Mrs. Carson agreed it was ready to mail to *St. Nicholas*.

Months went by without word from the magazine. Each month the disappointed girl checked her copy of *St. Nicholas* to see if the story appeared. The following September, Rachel opened the magazine and was overjoyed to see in print: "A Battle in the Clouds" by Rachel L. Carson. She received ten dollars from the magazine, a large payment for a young girl in 1917.

Rachel was now more determined than ever to be a real writer. She wrote and submitted another war story, which won a gold badge from *St. Nicholas* and was published in February 1919. A third story gained her honorary membership in the *St. Nicholas* League for student writers.

Rachel earned such good grades in school that she won a scholarship to the Pennsylvania College for Women. She still intended to pursue her career as a fiction writer. But in her second year of college, Rachel enrolled in a biology class only because it was required. She expected it to be as boring as high-school science. To her surprise, the class rekindled her love of nature. Rachel was so fascinated with biology that she decided to earn her degree in marine biology instead of in writing.

Rachel's classmates and professors were shocked. They told her that she was wasting her writing talent. At this time, women had achieved only modest civil rights in U.S. society. They had won the right to vote, but nobody believed a woman would be accepted as a scientist.

Rachel proved the world wrong. After college, she completed graduate work at Johns Hopkins University in Baltimore, Maryland. In 1935, she became the first woman scientist ever to be hired by the U.S. government. Her job combined her knowledge of the sea and her ability to write about science for the general public. She later wrote many magazine articles and books.

Rachel Carson's most famous book was *Silent Spring*, the first work to warn people around the world about the dangers of pesticides. Throughout her life, Rachel pursued the two vital interests she had developed as a young farmgirl—writing and preserving nature.

MARIA CALLAS
PROFESSIONAL OPERA SINGER
AT AGE SIXTEEN
1923–1977

aria Callas and her family were listening intently to a radio broadcast of an opera. When the soprano missed hitting some of her high notes, ten-year-old Maria started yelling at the radio. A family friend told the girl to be respectful. After all, the singer was a great star. "I don't care if she is a star," Maria raged. "She sings off-key. Just wait and see, one day I'm going to be a star myself, a bigger star than her."

Maria's mother, Evangelia, had always wanted her children to develop musical talent. Music reminded Evangelia of her home in Greece. After her baby son's death, the family attempted to start anew by moving to the United States. Maria and Cynthia Callas were both born in the United States, where Evangelia filled the house with radio music.

After George Callas bought his own drugstore, the family had enough money to buy a small piano and later a phonograph. Maria amazed her parents by naming the melodies her mother played. Soon the girl could sing every word of the songs. Maria was proving to be especially talented.

Maria began formal singing and piano lessons at age seven, and her sister started piano the same year, at age thirteen. Maria made tremendous strides and was becoming a truly talented singer. When Maria practiced her favorite opera arias, Evangelia saw crowds gathering on the street below. Neighbors would listen and applaud the young singer.

Despite Maria's obvious talent, her father disapproved of his daughters' music lessons. The Depression had struck, and his store had closed. Callas believed his daughters' music lessons were a luxury when money was scarce. Evangelia argued that life had been more comfortable in Greece. Caught between her parents' disagreements, Maria began to find music an ordeal. The moody girl stuffed herself with food to bury her unhappiness.

For many years, Maria said she wanted to be a dentist. Her mother would not listen to such talk. She grew up without toys, playtime, and friends so she could sing. As her voice matured, Evangelia dragged her daughter to perform at contests and on radio programs. The shy, sad girl hated these performances. But her mother insisted they were important for her career. Gradually, Maria became accustomed to audiences—enough to win top prizes at various major talent shows.

When Maria was thirteen, Evangelia decided to move with her daughters back to Greece. There the girls could have the advanced music training they needed. After leaving the United States, Maria had further formal education. She and her mother decided that singing was her destiny. Maria became as driven by singing as her mother.

Once in Greece, Evangelia paraded Maria before anyone who would listen. People enjoyed listening to the young girl, but few shared her mother's high hopes. Finally, Maria auditioned for a teacher at the National Conservatory of Athens. The school was for students sixteen and older. To gain entry for her thirteen-year-old daughter, Maria's mother lied about the girl's age. The unsuspecting teacher thought Maria so talented she arranged a scholarship for Maria.

Maria studied many hours a day at the conservatory for the next two years. She had no social life. She was completely controlled by the desire to be a great singer. Her sister, Cynthia, was a beautiful girl who had friends. Maria was overweight and unattractive, but she possessed the voice of the century.

In 1939, war broke out in Europe. When Italy and Germany conquered Greece, a celebrated Spanish singer, Elvira de Hidalgo, became stranded in Greece, there with no way to escape. Evangelia Callas decided that studying with this world-famous *prima donna* would be good for Maria's career.

Maria was nervous about auditioning for the well-known singer. At their first meeting, Elvira wondered why a girl who bit her fingernails and looked

so awkward wanted to perform. But when Maria sang, Elvira was amazed by her musical gift. Elvira could not resist the opportunity to train and perfect the teenager's wonderful voice. Elvira arranged for Maria to attend the leading music school in Athens, the Odeon Athena. She also offered to teach the girl for free.

Elvira became Maria's teacher, professional manager, and in many ways, her mother. From ten in the morning until late at night, Elvira trained Maria in drama and voice. She also helped boost the girl's confidence and taught her about clothes and how to wear her hair. Under Elvira's guidance, Maria was transformed from a girl with excellent talent to a young woman with remarkable skill and grace.

With Elvira's help, Maria entered the world of professional opera. Less than a year after her first roles with Greece's National Lyric Opera, Maria became a permanent member of that company. At age seventeen, she was the youngest person ever to join a European opera company.

Maria's big break came in 1941, when a lead singer at the Lyric suddenly became ill. The teenager played the beautiful Floria in the opera *Tosca*. Maria was a triumphant success. Critics praised her dramatic acting ability and her extraordinary, emotional singing.

Maria's acting and singing revolutionized modern opera. Some called Maria the "Golden Voice of the Century." All the years of pent-up emotions from her childhood went into her singing. And the little girl who vowed to be a singer kept her word. She became the biggest operatic star of the century.

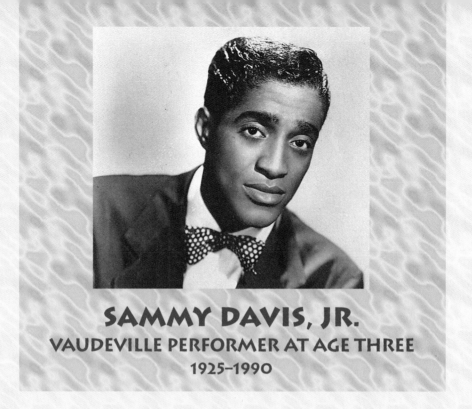

SAMMY DAVIS, JR.
VAUDEVILLE PERFORMER AT AGE THREE
1925–1990

n the vaudeville era of the early 1900s, variety shows featured singers, dancers, magicians, comedians, animal acts, and a vast array of other performers. Sometimes, entire families played the vaudeville circuit together.

That's the way it was for Elvera "Baby" Sanchez and Sammy Davis, Sr. The married couple lived in Harlem, but they spent a lot of time on the road with Will Mastin's traveling vaudeville show. Their son, Sammy Davis, Jr., grew up on the stage.

Shortly after Sammy's birth, his mother left him in the care of his grandmother so that Elvera could go back to work. When his parents separated, Sammy joined his father on the road. He adopted Will Mastin as his uncle.

At first, Sammy stayed backstage or at rooming houses while his father worked. One day, Will Mastin found Sammy playing with makeup and offered to show Sammy how to apply it properly. Will blacked Sammy's brown face and gave him large white lips. He looked like a tiny version of

Al Jolson, a singer who was popular in the 1920s.

Mastin got an idea for a cute act. He instructed an adult singer to perform Jolson's famous song, "Sonny Boy." Meanwhile, pint-sized Sammy sat on her lap made up like Jolson. Offstage, Mastin motioned to Sammy, instructing him to roll his eyes or make funny faces while the woman sang. Sammy pinched his nose during high notes, fluttered his lips as hers trembled, and heaved huge breaths as the singer gasped for air. The audience roared with laughter. When Sammy left the stage, Mastin said, "Listen to that applause, Sammy, some of it's for you." Sammy heard the applause. He wanted it to last forever.

Traveling with the vaudeville show, Sammy imitated anything he saw. One day, he joined the piano player as he rehearsed. The three-year-old amazed onlookers by repeating the entire hour-and-twenty-minute show, complete with songs, dances, and jokes. From then on, Sammy sang and danced in his father's act. He picked up their lightning-quick style of "flash dancing." The fancy steps won Sammy a silver cup and ten dollars in a dance contest with older children. The word spread about the talented youngster, and by age eight, Sammy had earned parts in two movies.

Show business was a hard life for the Will Mastin Trio. During the 1930s, Hollywood began producing movies with sound, or "talking pictures." This new entertainment attracted audiences away from vaudeville houses. At times, there were no jobs. They struggled to buy food and other necessities. That's when Sammy and his father went home to his Mama, the name Sammy gave his grandmother.

Sammy Davis, Jr., had no formal education. His school was the stage. If local social workers questioned his father about the child working so much, Sammy Sr. claimed the boy was a midget! Whenever he could afford it, Sammy Sr. found his son a tutor. But Sammy Jr. could not read much more than comic books until he grew up and joined the army. Then a sergeant taught Sammy to read books.

The most bitter battle Sammy Davis, Jr., fought was against racism. When he traveled as a young performer, his father protected him from white people's ugly insults and rules. When Sammy Jr. joined the army at age eighteen, he learned how much hatred some people held toward him—just because of skin color. He now understood why the Will Mastin Trio had not become bigger stars. Sammy decided to "dance down the barriers" between him and his audiences. He was even more determined to be a star.

After entertaining troops in the army, Sammy rejoined the group that was now called "The Will Mastin Trio, Featuring Sammy Davis, Jr." By this time, the trio was largely a showcase for the younger Davis's incredible talent. Sammy had taught himself to play piano, drums, trumpet, and vibes. The group made a slow climb to the top.

As their fame spread, Sammy Davis, Jr., began making records and starring in movies, plays, and on television. He became a pioneer in entertainment, breaking down barriers for other African-American artists to follow. He was one of the first African-Americans to host his own television show and to own a share of a Las Vegas hotel.

Sammy Davis, Jr., displayed great courage as an entertainer. His contributions to humane causes earned him many awards, honorary degrees from black colleges. He was honored in the NAACP Hall of Fame. The talents that little Sammy Davis, Jr., developed as a child made the adult entertainer one of the most revered and adored performers of his time.

BETTY MARIE TALLCHIEF (MARIA TALLCHIEF PASCHEN)
BALLERINA AT AGE TWELVE
1925–

Ruth Tallchief watched her daughter dancing around their home. To the mother, it seemed that the girl moved in rhythm to music playing inside her head. Indeed, Elizabeth Marie Tallchief, called "Betty Marie" by her family, loved the feel of her body in motion to music.

As a very young child, Betty Marie learned many different kinds of dancing. Her father was Alexander Tallchief, a full-blooded Osage Indian. Her grandfather was Chief Big Heart, an Osage leader. Young Betty Marie loved to watch her tribespeople celebrate special occasions to rhythmic drums and shaking gourds. She was equally fascinated by the Scotch-Irish tunes from her mother's heritage.

When she was just three years old, Betty Marie could repeat drumbeats on the piano. Her mother took this as a sign that her daughter had unusual memory and musical talents, so she arranged piano lessons for the girl. The piano teacher agreed that Betty Marie possessed perfect pitch. When Ruth

Tallchief saw how moving to music delighted her daughter, she enrolled Betty Marie in dance classes as well.

As a youngster, Betty Marie's days were filled with lessons and practicing. Once she began school, the little girl was busy from dawn until sundown. She rose early to practice piano before breakfast. After school, she played piano again for an hour. Her mother preferred piano over dance. So Betty Marie had to practice piano many hours before she was free to dance or play.

News of Betty Marie's unusual talent spread quickly. Civic leaders asked her to perform at local functions. Betty Marie danced, played piano, or sometimes did both. After her younger sister, Marjorie, began dance lessons, they entertained together. Before long, the girls had surpassed their teachers' skills. Ruth Tallchief decided to move the family to Los Angeles. There, Betty Marie and Marjorie received advanced ballet training. Betty Marie continued piano lessons at the Los Angeles Conservatory of Music.

Ruth Tallchief was sure her daughter would be a concert pianist. Betty Marie felt torn between piano and dance. Then her dance teacher selected her to perform with the Los Angeles Light Opera Company chorus line. Dancing on a real stage in front of a live audience convinced the twelve-year-old that she wanted to become a ballerina.

Betty Marie danced with the opera company throughout high school. At the same time, she trained with famous choreographers and dancers. Betty Marie responded to their demands for higher standards. In turn, they gave her opportunities to display her graceful skills.

When Betty Marie was sixteen, the manager of the famous Ballet Russe asked her to tour with the company. Betty Marie was overjoyed. But her mother wanted her to finish high school and go to college. Betty Marie obeyed her mother and completed high school.

The summer after she graduated, the Ballet Russe repeated its job offer. This time, her mother agreed to allow her daughter enter the world of professional ballet. By signing this first contract, Betty Marie began her rapid climb to become one of the world's greatest ballerinas.

Betty Marie's tireless will, great talent, and quick memory earned her a permanent place in the Ballet Russe. During her five years with the company, Betty Marie went from a rarely seen standby to performing leading roles. Critics raved about her graceful style, and audiences loved her youthful radiance. Betty Marie adopted the stage name "Maria Tallchief" and continued her brilliant career as prima ballerina with the New York City Ballet. She later founded the Chicago School of Ballet. Her outstanding talent brought her honors from around the world.

Perhaps her most important tribute came from the Osage Indians in Fairfax, Oklahoma, where Maria was born. The tribe held a ceremony with great feasting and songs composed especially for her. At the close of the celebration, Maria received a beautiful Osage costume with a beaded crown. From then on, Maria was called Princess *Wa-Xthe-Thonba*, or "Princess of Two Standards." The name recognized that Maria belonged to two worlds—the Osages and her mother's people of European descent. Both worlds merged in the life of a little girl who loved to dance.

SHIRLEY TEMPLE
MOVIE STAR AT AGE THREE
1928–

Shirley Temple was born one year before the beginning of the Great Depression, a time when the United States economy fell into ruin. Many rich people lost their fortunes, and the less wealthy sank into poverty. Families of unemployed workers joined breadlines across the country. Meanwhile, Hollywood attempted to produce movies that would cheer up the discouraged nation. Shirley Temple proved to be the ideal young entertainer to help unhappy people forget their troubles.

Shirley began dance classes when she was three years old at Mrs. Meglin's Dance Studio near the Temples' Santa Monica, California, home. After a few months, a movie director spotted Shirley and thought she would be perfect for his series of short comedy films called *Baby Burlesk*. The films were imitations of popular adult movies, but starred kids in the adult roles. In various features, little Shirley portrayed a French girl, Tarzan's Jane, and many other characters. She earned fifty dollars a week, a sizable sum during the Depression.

Shirley loved to sing and dance, and she learned unusually quickly. She could see a dance step or hear her lines once and repeat them perfectly. During the next few years, film crews called her "One-Take Temple." This meant that she was able to perform her songs and dances perfectly, and there was rarely a need for a second run-through, or "take."

Making movies was hard work, especially for a spirited four-year-old. Hours were long and rules strict. At Shirley's first studio, children who caused trouble were ordered into a large black box as punishment. The scary box had little fresh air and contained a large block of melting ice. This made the muddy floor an impossible place to sit. There were days when Shirley alternated between standing for long periods in the cold box and acting under hot lights. The combination of extreme temperatures, dampness, and long workdays often made Shirley sick. But the studio only cared about finishing movies on schedule. So Shirley worked with ear infections, fevers, and cuts.

Within a year, the studio went bankrupt. By then, Shirley had completed eight *Baby Burlesks*, five short comedies, and seven smaller parts. She was five years old, too young for kindergarten, and out of work.

Shirley's next big break came when a new movie studio gave her a major role in the film *Stand up and Cheer*. The curly-haired, dimpled youngster was an instant success. She starred in six more movies that same year, establishing her as a celebrity. The film studio offered her parents a seven-year contract. Producers prepared more movies featuring Shirley as a spunky, appealing orphan who solved problems to win the hearts of adults. With each film, Shirley's lively, brave personality attracted more Depression-weary fans.

After *Little Miss Marker* became a major hit, Shirley Temple was famous around the world. Manufacturers put her face and name on toys, books, clothes, and records. Fan clubs sprang up everywhere. In the United States, she became known as "America's Sweetheart." South Americans referred to Shirley as *Ricito de Oro*, or "Golden Curls." Four thousand fan letters a week arrived at the Temple home. In 1935, she received a special Academy Award—the first Oscar® ever awarded to a child. Shirley's plaque read:

> *The award is bestowed because Shirley Temple brought*
> *more happiness to millions of children and grown-ups than*
> *any other child of her years in the history of the world.*

When she was nine years of age, Shirley earned about $307,000, the seventh-largest annual salary in the United States. Shirley's father quit his bank job to manage her career.

Fame and fortune had its price, however. Fans, eager to touch her or grab a lock of hair, mobbed her everywhere. Writers and photographers reported her every move. The studio tried to shield her by hiding her from the public. When Shirley stopped appearing in public, rumors circulated that she had been kidnapped for ransom. All the time, she was simply working long hours at the studio. She grew lonely and bored.

By the time Shirley entered her teens, her popularity had faded. People did not find the cute smile of a thirteen-year-old nearly as adorable as that of a six-year-old. For a few years, Shirley made movies and hosted television shows. But her days as a superstar had ended.

The adult Shirley Temple left show business and entered politics. In 1967, she won a seat in the United States House of Representatives. Two years later, President Richard Nixon appointed her the United States delegate to the United Nations. Other honors followed. President Gerald Ford named Shirley Temple Black (her married name) as ambassador to Ghana. When Ford brought her back to the White House in 1976, he named her Chief of Protocol. She became the first woman to claim the title. In 1990, President George Bush sent Black to her most challenging post as ambassador to the troubled country of Czechoslovakia.

In the Depression, little Shirley Temple charmed the world in a dark and hopeless time. The adult Shirley Temple Black has continued to serve the public in vital and important ways.

— Shirley Temple Black with a doll from the 1930s, when she was a child movie star. —

CHILD STARS IN EARLY HOLLYWOOD

Being a child star in the 1920s, 1930s, and 1940s was a dream come true for a select, few children. Bright lights, applause, and luxury living—these were the attractions that lured children and their parents into show business. And large sums of money kept them there.

Few people imagined the difficult lives young stars endured in order to have their names on theater marquees. Family life often suffered when there was a young showperson in the house. Child stars frequently earned more money than their parents, which caused hard feelings. In addition, performing youngsters required more of their parents' time at odd hours of the day for tryouts, filming, and late-night performances. Every time the child went on the road, the family separated as a parent or other adult had to accompany the child.

Until the 1930s, child stars labored long hours. Young actors spent most of their nonperforming time in their dressing rooms. They had to be near the set for makeup, costume fittings, or last-minute directions. Studios signed the actors to binding contracts, and they controlled the children's every movement. The kids were told how to act, what to eat, and even whom to date.

Judy Garland's personality was ill-suited for the stress of stardom. The studio's pressures on her eventually destroyed her life. Judy first sang onstage when she was just two years old. After playing many bit parts in movies, she got her big break at age fifteen. Judy landed the starring role of Dorothy in *The Wizard of Oz*. The movie was a huge hit, and it is still loved by children and adults many generations after its 1939 release.

— *Judy Garland* —

For the next thirteen years, Judy Garland displayed her incredible talents on-screen as a musical actress. But her studio, M-G-M, required her to work an extremely busy schedule. She was given all sorts of drugs—pills to keep her from gaining weight; pills to help her sleep; pills to wake her up for morning filming. By the time she was twenty-eight, Judy was hopelessly addicted to drugs. For Judy Garland, a bright beginning as a child star ended in a tragic, early ruin. She died at age forty-seven from an overdose of sleeping pills.

Young **Mickey Rooney** thrived on his Hollywood upbringing. Mickey made his movie debut at age six, playing a midget in a 1926 movie entitled *Not To Be Trusted*. By the time he was seventeen years old, the gifted actor had a string of huge box-office hits. He starred in fifteen "Hardy Family" movies that became the most successful series in film history, earning Mickey a special Oscar® at age nineteen.

Despite his busy acting schedule, Mickey claims he had a normal childhood. "I had everything a kid should have—and more. I not only studied, but played football, tennis, and other games."

Throughout his early career, Mickey attended a studio school. His classmates were other famous child actors, such as Judy Garland and Elizabeth Taylor. Young **Elizabeth Taylor** seemed to enjoy the bright lights, too. At nine years of age, she had come to California with her family, and she quickly landed a movie contract with Universal Pictures in 1941. Two years later, the wide-eyed eleven-year-old played a leading role

— Mickey Rooney —

in *Lassie Come Home*. The next year, Elizabeth charmed audiences across the country in *National Velvet*. From then on, Elizabeth enjoyed a long career as one of America's most beloved actresses.

Child stars such as Taylor, Rooney, and Garland earned thousands of dollars a week. This was in the 1930s, when the average adult earned just $474 a year! Yet the youngsters rarely had any control over their salaries.

— Elizabeth Taylor —

Their parents handled their money and gave their talented children small allowances.

One child actor, **Jackie Coogan**, raked in millions. In addition to his huge acting salary, Jackie earned money by lending his name to products. There were Jackie Coogan dolls, erector sets, lunch pails, and chocolates. Money from royalties earned the boy $10 million.

Shortly after his father died, Jackie's mother married his business manager. That's when Jackie discovered that his mother had been mishandling his earnings. She had spent $2 million within two years after his father's death. Jackie Coogan became the first child to sue his parents in court. And he was the first child performer to fight for protection of money earned

— *Jackie Coogan* —

while underage. In 1939, the California governor signed what became known as the "Coogan Law." The law was the first step toward protecting children's money from parents' mishandling. It also signaled the beginning of concern for the rights of child performers.

Child labor laws brought some controls on the amount of time a studio could work a child. The laws also required that young performers receive three hours of schooling each workday. Studios hired tutors who either coordinated assignments from the children's schools or instructed the youngsters directly. Sometimes, a child actor was the only student in a studio classroom. One teacher taught all the subjects.

ANNE FRANK
AUTHOR OF WARTIME DIARY
AT AGE THIRTEEN
1929–1945

I want to go on living even after my death! And therefore I
am grateful to God for giving me this gift, this possibility
of developing myself and of writing, of expressing all that
is in me. I can shake off everything if I write; my sorrows
disappear, my courage is reborn.

— Anne Frank
Tuesday, April 4, 1944

Anne Frank received a diary for her thirteenth birthday. At the time, she was thrilled at the prospect of having a secret friend with whom she could share her most private thoughts. Anne never imagined that that this diary would keep her from going mad. It would also become the world's most vivid account of life for Jews hiding from German Nazis during World War II.

Anne, her parents, and older sister, Margot, were familiar with religious hatred because they were Jewish. In Frankfurt-am-Main, Germany, where she was born, Chancellor Adolf Hitler had instituted many anti-Jewish laws. Hitler defended his actions by declaring pure Germans a superior race. He proclaimed all other peoples were inferior, especially Jews.

To escape from Hitler, the Franks moved to Amsterdam, the Netherlands, when Anne was four. For a few years, Anne and her sister led normal and happy lives. They attended school and played with friends. But when Hitler's army began invading European countries in 1939, the safety of Jews everywhere was at risk.

Germany attacked the Netherlands in 1940, and with the army came anti-Jewish laws from Adolf Hitler. One by one, freedoms disappeared for Jews like Anne Frank and her family. Jews were commanded to wear yellow, six-pointed stars as identification. Laws prohibited Jews from going to theaters, public sports centers, and schools. Anyone who protested these injustices was sent to work camps or concentration camps. Few people ever returned from these prisons.

When sixteen-year-old Margot Frank received "call-up papers" for one of these camps, the family decided to act quickly. On July 9, 1942, thirteen-year-old Anne put on many layers of vests, pants, stockings, and other outerwear. Her family was going into hiding. They could take only as much clothing as they could wear. Anne packed hair curlers, schoolbooks, a comb, old letters, and, of course, her diary into a bag. She realized some people might think she was strange for bringing these items into hiding. "But I'm not sorry," she wrote that night in her diary. "Memories mean more to me than dresses."

After saying good-bye to her cat, who went to a neighbor, Anne left with her family in the morning rain. The family walked to Mr. Frank's office. Hidden behind a door at the top of a staircase, a secret hiding place had been built. There was a room large enough for Mr. and Mrs. Frank's bedroom, a smaller room for Margot and Anne, and a bathroom. Up another flight of stairs was a makeshift kitchen with a stove. There also were two more rooms for another Jewish family, the Van Daans, and their fifteen-year-old son, Peter. Later, a dentist named Albert Dussel joined the group in their cramped quarters. By then, a movable bookcase hid the entrance to the secret apartment.

The only people Anne saw were two men and two women office workers who secretly brought them food, books, and newspapers. During the day, several workers occupied the office below, so Anne and the others bare-ly moved for hours at a time. One footstep could make a floorboard creak. Any little noise could give them away. Even flushing the toilet had to wait until all the employees left for the day. If anyone suspected there were Jews hiding in the attic, they might inform the Nazis. Anne and her companions lived in fear that at any moment, Nazi soldiers would arrive to cart them off to certain death.

For the next two years, Anne wrote in her diary about the oppressive life in what she called the "Secret Annex." She described the

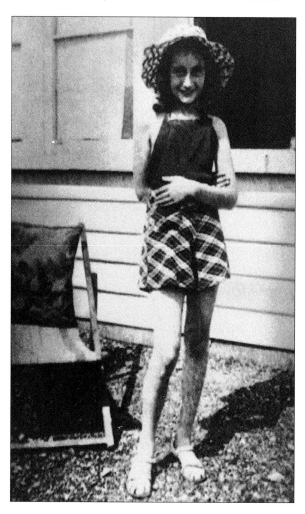

loneliness and isolation of being cut off from the rest of the world. And she detailed the scary drama she observed through their hideout window. She saw entire Jewish families being rounded up and forced to board trains. These trains, she knew, were headed for concentration camps.

Anne's writings explored deeper feelings than the nightmares of her ordeal. Anne Frank revealed in her diary a sensitive teenager coming of age during troubled times—her loves and longings, and her search for independence from her parents. Page after page, Anne's spirit and intelligence rose above the degrading conditions of her imprisonment.

Anne's diary ended on August 4, 1944. On that day, German security police raided the attic hideout. All eight lodgers were arrested and sent to concentration camps. Anne and Margot died of typhus at the Bergen-Belsen camp two months before friendly troops freed the Netherlands. Of the eight who hid together, Anne's father was the only survivor.

After the war, Mr. Frank returned to Amsterdam. He discovered that a woman who had helped his family was able to recover some possessions from the hideout. Among the papers was Anne's diary. Otto Frank decided that the best memorial to his daughter would be to publish her story. *Anne Frank: The Diary of a Young Girl* has sold more than thirteen million copies in fifty languages since its first printing in 1947. The journal is acknowledged as one of the most important wartime records. Equally important, Anne's diary stands as a monument to the courageous spirit of youth in the most vicious and threatening situations.

THE QUIZ KIDS

The early 1940s were chaotic years in the United States and abroad. World War II raged in Europe, Africa, and Asia. The United States tried to stay out of the war and to revive a depressed economy. Most people worked hard, received small paychecks, and hoped for better times.

During this period, a popular means of affordable entertainment was the radio. Children longed for school days to end so they could rush home and listen to radio shows, such as "Superman" and "The Lone Ranger." Every night, families crowded around the radio to hear news, dramas, comedy, and music.

When radio was in its prime, a new form of show hit the airwaves—the quiz show. One of the most unusual and celebrated quiz shows was a program called "Quiz Kids," which featured children who were very smart. For thirty minutes each Sunday, four or five bright children were broadcast answering questions. Children with the top three scores returned the next week for another round of questions.

To be on "Quiz Kids," children completed a detailed questionnaire about school activities, hobbies, goals, and favorite books, and they wrote a 250-word essay about why they wanted to be a Quiz Kid. Once applicants were accepted, they went through auditions to see how they would act on the show.

Questions came from listeners who tried to stump the kids. For every selected question that a Quiz Kid answered correctly, the sender won a radio. For incorrect answers, senders got radio-phonographs. Quiz Kids earned a one-hundred-dollar United States savings bond each time they were on the show, a large amount in the 1940s.

"Quiz Kids" was an overnight success. Within ten months of its debut, reviewers acclaimed it as the best children's show on radio and one of the more interesting shows overall. Soon it had a loyal following of nearly twenty million listeners. Appealing, brainy children were just what Americans needed to take their minds off food rationing and war. Favorite Quiz Kids who were good at answering questions came back again and again to an admiring audience. In everyday life, people began calling a smart person a "quiz kid."

Students on "Quiz Kids" became celebrities. The show's creator, Louis G. Cowan, insisted that his stars were merely "bright kids who had unusual hobbies and preferred encyclopedias to comic books." Indeed, many Quiz Kids didn't know that Superman was Clark Kent, a fact that most children of the 1940s knew from reading comic books. But the nation expected great things of children such as Gerard Darrow, the youngest Quiz Kid. By age four, Gerard could identify one hundred birds. Naomi Cooks, a pig-tailed seven-year-old, quoted from Greek mythology and the Bible.

— *Quiz Kids Harve Bennett, Richard Williams, Joel Kupperman, and Ruth Duskin (left to right)*
—

The Quiz Kids traveled coast-to-coast with the show as "ambassadors of goodwill." The youngsters won a Treasury Department medal for helping sell $118 million in savings bonds after the United States entered World War II in 1941. The Quiz Kids also participated in collecting scrap metal and rubber, and planting victory gardens, as did many other children of that time. After the war, Quiz Kids raised money for causes such as the Red Cross, the March of Dimes, and relief for war-torn France. Sometimes, Quiz Kids were on the road with their guardians and a stack of school homework for weeks. And everywhere they went, they dazzled adults with their cleverness. By the late 1940s, television was beginning to overtake radio. Foreseeing television's future popularity, many radio stars switched to the new medium. In 1949, "Quiz Kids" debuted on television. The young scholars wore caps and gowns that caused them to sweat under hot television lights. For the next few years, the show remained as popular as it had been on radio. But by 1954, interest in the Quiz Kids had waned.

After the show ended, its graduates were faced with the challenge of shifting to a normal lifestyle after spending years as radio and television stars.

One former Quiz Kid who achieved great success in adult life was Harve Bennett Fischman. Young Harve earned a reputation for his unusually good memory and intense interest in history long before he joined "Quiz Kids." When he was a very young boy, his mother read him a book called *Boyhood Adventures of Our Presidents*. Several days later, Harve shocked everyone at a birthday party when he recited from memory the names of all the United States presidents.

Harve's Chicago public school was part of a pilot program to test a new teaching method—reading by memorizing words from flash cards. Once Harve saw a word, he never forgot it. He became the school's fastest flashcard reader and completed the first year of reading instruction in only two weeks. As a Quiz Kid, Harve amazed audiences with rare history facts about presidents and their wives and Civil War battles. His likable, clever personality won over everyone on the show, and Harve Bennett fan clubs sprouted up across the country. In his hometown of Chicago, Harve began a professional writing career. The Chicago *Sun-Times* offered him a regular column when he was just fourteen years old. "Hi-Lites by Harve" was a newsy column about events in Chicago high schools. It was a unique column because in those days, major newspapers did not cover high-school sports and other activities.

After graduation from "Quiz Kids" at age sixteen, Harve found it difficult to come down from his celebrity status and lead a normal life. He admitted that it took him twenty years to recover from what he called "pursuing the applause addiction." But his experience on stage plus an intense interest in movies gave him direction. As an adult, Harve produced and wrote many top network shows, including "The Six Million Dollar Man" and "The Bionic Woman." At one point in the 1970s, four of Harve Bennett's TV shows were ranked first, second, third, and fifth in national ratings. Later, he was a producer for several of the "Star Trek" movies.

Harve Bennett was not the only former Quiz Kid who succeeded after the television show ended. Most Quiz Kids continued to excel in school. Many eventually made names for themselves in various fields—as educators (Margaret Merrick Scheffelin, Joel Kupperman), authors (Ruth Duskin Feldman), scientists (Nobel prizewinner James Watson), and actors (Vanessa Brown). For these and other former Quiz Kids, their star qualities as children shone in their adult lives, as well.

JIM HENSON
TELEVISION PUPPETEER AT AGE SEVENTEEN
1937–1990

J ames Maury Henson's earliest memories of puppets were from the radio. Oddly enough, puppets could not be seen on radio. Nevertheless, ventriloquist Edgar Bergen delighted an entire generation of children by performing on radio with puppets named Charlie McCarthy and Mortimer Snerd. Young Jim Henson would sit before the radio and imagine the hilarious exploits suggested by these voices. To the young boy, Charlie McCarthy and Mortimer Snerd seemed like real people.

Then, in the 1950s, television entered millions of American homes. Jim became fascinated with the television show "Kukla, Fran, and Ollie." On this show, the puppeteer hid behind a platform as he moved and spoke for the hand puppets Kukla and Ollie, who joked with a woman named Fran. Jim watched the show all the time. He joined the puppet club at his new high school in suburban Washington, D.C.

Even more than puppetry, television fascinated Jim Henson. When he was old enough to work, the teen applied to all the television stations in

Washington. Soon he heard that one station needed a puppeteer. Jim and a friend constructed Pierre, a French rat, and some cowboy puppets for the audition. They got a job on "The Junior Morning Show."

Although the show lasted only three weeks, Jim's act received good newspaper reviews. His puppets attracted enough attention to land him a job with the NBC television network on a local cartoon program. As his television career progressed, Jim enrolled at the University of Maryland to study art. In college, he learned about staging, set design, and, of course, puppetry. After a year in college, the eighteen-year-old was offered his own television show by Washington, D.C., television station WRC.

Jim's show was called "Sam and His Friends," and it was allotted a brief five minutes late at night. But those five minutes were enough to launch a brilliant career. With help from another puppetry student, Jane Nebel (Jim's future wife), Jim constructed several new puppet characters, including Kermit the Frog. With Kermit, Jim reenacted scenes from his youth. Kermit fished for frogs in the creek and rode horses through peaceful countrysides, just as Jim and a childhood friend named Kermit had done.

Jim Henson proved to be a genius at bringing puppets alive on television and, eventually, in film. His "Muppets" were soft, rather than wooden, which allowed for flexible facial expressions. By not attaching marionette strings, he was able to hide the Muppets' controls from television viewers. Jim used close-up camera angles to show the Muppets' emotions.

By the late 1960s, Jim Henson had become known as the leading puppeteer in the world. In 1969, he was hired to create characters for the new public television children's show, "Sesame Street." In addition to Kermit the Frog, Jim's creations of Big Bird, Oscar the Grouch, and the Cookie Monster have entertained and educated millions of children in eighty countries for decades. Jim Henson's fame fueled his creativity. "The Muppet Show" of the 1970s inspired several Muppet movies, and, later, "The Muppet Babies." Jim then produced two fantasy films, *The Dark Crystal* and *Labyrinth*, and added his technical skills to make the film *Teenage Mutant Ninja Turtles* a hit. Today, the Muppets are sold as toys and are pictured on lunchboxes, clothing, and countless other products for kids.

Jim Henson died suddenly at the age of fifty-three in 1990. The entire world mourned the mild-mannered genius. He may not have been the first puppeteer on television, but he was the first to apply video technology to enhance the charm of puppets.

PELÉ
(EDSON ARANTES DO NASCIMENTO)
PROFESSIONAL SOCCER STAR AT AGE FIFTEEN
1940–

Edson Arantes do Nascimento always loved soccer, the sport most of the world calls "football" (or *futbol* in Spanish-speaking countries). Edson's earliest memories were of watching his father, Dondinho do Nascimento, play professional Brazilian soccer for the Bauru Atletico Club. After his father's games, Edson played soccer with neighborhood friends and amazed them by imitating his father's skillful moves. It wasn't long before Edson Arantes do Nascimento was known around the world as Pelé, the greatest soccer player of all time.

Young Edson lived with his parents, siblings, uncle, and grandmother in a three-room house. Their home was in Bauru, a town in southern Brazil. Although Dondinho was a good soccer player, he made the equivalent of five U.S. dollars for each soccer game, a small amount for a man trying to support a family. Dondinho supplemented his income by working as an aide at the state health clinic .

Initially, the family downplayed the importance of soccer. Celeste was opposed to her children following her husband's path. She feared that they would be injured or remain poor if they pursued the sport professionally. But Edson seemed to have soccer in his blood. He always found a way to sneak into the street for a game with his friends. Edson could go to school, shine shoes at the railroad station, help his father at the clinic, and still find time to play soccer.

Edson and the other boys were too poor to afford a soccer ball. Instead, they made one from a sock stuffed with rags and crumpled newspapers. They played on the unpaved street in front of Edson's house. It took extra skill to direct the oddly shaped ball through potholes and mud puddles. Still, Edson played better than much older boys. Teammates would cheer, "Pelé! Pelé!" when he kicked a goal. Edson says he never knew why they chose that nickname—he doesn't even know what the word means. Nevertheless, the name stuck.

Pelé began school when he was eight. School was never his favorite activity. He spent much of the day getting into mischief or wishing for the day to end so he could play soccer.

Shortly after starting school, Pelé and his friends organized a soccer team with real equipment. The boys asked their mothers to sew shorts from flour sacks. They scraped together money to buy jerseys. They collected enough soccer trading cards to trade in for a real soccer ball. The group called themselves the September 7th Club after Brazil's Independence Day. However, the team usually referred to themselves as "the shoeless ones." They often played barefoot because they were too poor to own shoes.

Pelé's teammates elected him team captain. After a few days of practice, September 7th competed with other neighborhood teams. During the next few years, September 7th won every game it played. When the mayor sponsored a local soccer tournament, nearly five thousand fans jammed the stadium for the championship game. This was the first time Pelé played on a real soccer field. September 7th easily defeated the other team. When Pelé scored the game's final goal, the crowd chanted "Pelé! Pelé! Pelé!" People threw money on the field, and Pelé's teammates gave it all to him since he was the game's *artilheiro*, or "leading scorer."

Pelé stayed with the team for about five years. Then he played for a youth club organized by his father's professional team. After finishing secondary school at age fourteen, Pelé devoted even more energy to soccer. But he also had to earn money. He sewed boots in a shoe factory and worked in a dry-cleaning store. All the time, Pelé's soccer skills were improving, and he was beginning to be noticed by professional scouts. When Pelé was fifteen, he was offered a contract with the Santos Soccer Club of Sao Paulo, Brazil.

Pelé played briefly for the Santos second-string team. His lightning kicks and constant scoring convinced the coaches to start him on the first team. By the end of his first year with the Santos, the teenage Pelé scored a remarkable sixty-seven goals in seventy-five games.

That summer Pelé was selected to play with Brazil's national team in the 1958 World Cup, the most important soccer tournament in the world. The seventeen-year-old led Brazil to World Cup victory—Brazil's first World Cup title ever. Now the world knew of Brazil's young soccer superstar.

This was just the beginning of Pelé's twenty-two-year professional soccer career. During that time, he played for Santos and the Brazilian national team. In the 1970s, he joined the New York Cosmos of the North American Soccer League. Pelé scored more goals than any player in the world—1,281 goals in 1,363 professional games. He also led Brazil to two more World Cup championships in 1962 and 1970, becoming the only person ever to play on three World Cup championship teams.

Pelé's fame was so great that kings, queens, prime ministers, and presidents from around the world came to see him play and shake his hand. Once, the African nation of Nigeria declared a two-day truce in its war with Biafra so both sides could watch Pelé play. Songs, movies, and books celebrate the success of Pelé, one of the greatest athletes in the history of sports.

WILMA RUDOLPH
OLYMPIC RUNNER AT AGE SIXTEEN
1940–1994

Wilma Rudolph was born in Clarksville, Tennessee, the twentieth of Blanche and Eddie Rudolph's twenty-two children. The Rudolphs were the kind of parents who encouraged their children when others said to give up. They inspired Wilma to fight from the day of her birth.

Little Wilma was born at a dangerously low weight. Doctors told the Rudolphs that their daughter had little chance to survive. But the infant weathered her rough start, as well as a series of critical illnesses throughout her childhood. The most serious threat to Wilma's life was a bout with polio. Wilma survived, but the disease had hampered her ability to walk. Doctors said she would need crutches for the rest of her life. Blanche Rudolph refused to listen. She bundled her four-year-old daughter in a blanket and traveled 90 miles (145 km) round-trip by bus each week for physical therapy. And every night after dinner, she massaged Wilma's twisted leg. At the end of a year, Wilma showed slight improvement.

Blanche Rudolph believed that if the family worked together, Wilma would make greater progress. Three older children helped her take turns massaging Wilma's leg. Wilma sometimes tired of being poked and rubbed, but she never lost the courage to try to walk.

Finally, after two years, Wilma did walk. At first, she fell often. The determined girl only laughed and pulled herself up again. By age eight, Wilma was walking so well that her doctors fitted her with a leg brace. Later she wore a special high-topped shoe. Wilma was still unsteady, but she was able to go to school, and she could enjoy some of the games her classmates played.

At home, Wilma joined her brothers' basketball games. Whenever they played, Wilma was there to shoot, dribble, and run with the ball. Wilma became so interested in the sport that she continued practicing long after the boys had finished. One day, the confident girl decided to kick off her shoes and play in bare feet. From then on, Wilma never wore her special shoe again. "I felt at that point that my life was beginning at last," she later recalled.

With practice, Wilma's walking and jumping progressed to running— running faster than most boys and girls in her class. By the time she reached high school, the once-clumsy girl had grown into a tall, slender young woman with grace and speed. Her basketball coach nicknamed her "Skeeter" because she dashed and darted across the court with the frenzied speed of a mosquito. Wilma won all-state honors as a high-school basketball star. She set girl's state basketball records by scoring 803 points in 25 games.

At the same time, Wilma became a dominant track-and-field star, regularly taking first place at track meets in the 50-, 75-, and 100-yard dashes. She was so good that she was selected to be a member of the U.S. Olympics team at the 1956 Summer Olympic Games in Australia. Just a teenager, she ran on the U.S. women's 400-meter relay team and helped win the third-place bronze medal.

Four years later, the 1960 Olympics in Rome belonged to Wilma Rudolph. There, she became the first American woman to win three gold medals. She immediately was revered as the greatest woman athlete of her generation. Her heart-rending story of recovering from childhood polio made her an even more compelling hero to children and adults alike. In 1974, Wilma was inducted into the Black Athletes Hall of Fame. Ten years later, she was selected as one of five sports figures named America's Greatest Women Athletes.

After retiring from active competition, Wilma became a teacher and coach. She also founded the Wilma Rudolph Foundation. Through this organization, she encouraged sports-minded boys and girls to develop the same enthusiasm that drove her to stand, walk, and run.

SKATERS AND GYMNASTS: YOUNG GIRLS, OLYMPIC HEROES

Like Wilma Rudolph, many other young girls reach the highest level of athletic competition, the Olympics. In two sports—ice skating and gymnastics—girls, rather than grown women, have set championship standards for several decades.

Some seven decades after she won her first Olympic medal, **Sonja Henie** is still Norway's most famous athlete. Sonja was always determined to do everything first. She was the first figure skater to win three consecutive gold medals (in 1928, 1932, and 1936). She revolutionized the sport by becoming the first to add music and choreography to her skating routines. She also was the first to compete in a fancy costume.

— Sonja Henie —

Sonja's first Olympic competition was in 1924, when she was just twelve years old. She didn't win a gold medal then, but her father complained that the judges had not taken her seriously because of her age. Sonja came back and dominated world figure skating for more than a decade. She is still recognized as one of the sport's legends.

— Midori Ito —

— Kristi Yamaguchi —

Many young figure-skating stars have come and gone since Sonja Henie's day. Today's top skaters seem to get younger, yet more athletically skilled than their predecessors. **Midori Ito** thrilled the world in the late 1980s with her incredible jumps. In 1988, she became the first female skater to complete a gravity-defying triple axle in competition. Born in Nahoya, Japan, Midori has been skating since her tenth birthday. Early in her career, she faced the challenge of having to practice on her local rink, which was smaller than competition rinks. But she practiced tirelessly and perfected her jumps.

Going into the 1992 Olympics, Midori was one of the favorites to win the gold medal. But as well as she skated, she could manage only a second-place silver medal. Midori could not top the amazing **Kristi Yamaguchi**. Kristi is a Japanese-American teenager who grew up in California. Her performance enchanted the judges. Her gold medal made her an immediate star, and perhaps the most famous Japanese-American athlete ever. She even had her picture on a Wheaties box!

— *Olga Korbut* —

For many, figure skating is the highlight of the Winter Olympics. But dramatic gymnastics competitions draw the big crowds at the Summer Olympic Games. In recent years, "women's" gymnastics has been dominated by incredibly fit and agile teenage girls.

Olga Korbut dazzled audiences at the 1972 Olympics in Munich, Germany. The plucky girl from the Soviet Union collected three gold medals and became a worldwide celebrity. After the Olympics, she traveled the globe, meeting presidents, kings, and queens.

For the next four years, nobody thought a gymnast would top Olga Korbut's achievement. But in the very next Summer Olympics, an even younger girl from Romania did just that. Fourteen-year-old **Nadia Comaneci** had studied gymnastics with coach Bela Karolyi ever since she was six. At the 1976 Olympics, the quiet girl jumped up on the balance beam and stunned the world with a flawless performance. She received a perfect score of 10.0, the first female gymnast ever to do so. Nadia returned to the Olympics in 1980 and dominated once again, winning two gold and two silver medals.

— *Nadia Comaneci* —

— *Mary Lou Retton* —

Next it was an American's turn for perfection. At the 1984 Olympics in Los Angeles, home crowds filled the arena with a deafening chant of "U-S-A! U-S-A!" Who was the cause of this commotion? An energetic dynamo named **Mary Lou Retton**. This ever-cheerful sixteen-year-old scored a perfect 10.0 on her way to the all-around gold medal in women's gymnastics.

When athletes achieve perfection and win championships at young ages, they reach an unforgettable peak in life. For some, however, the struggle to achieve gold medals can be too much. The public is now learning of disturbing examples of young girls who train too hard. This places too much strain on their developing bodies. Some young girls become obsessed with staying thin, and they develop deadly eating disorders such as anorexia. Parents and coaches now are being advised to emphasize to young athletes that winning is not the only reason to participate in sports. We think of gold medals as the "ultimate"; but physical fitness, fun, and fair competition are the true, ultimate goals of sports.

SUSAN ELOISE HINTON
AUTHOR AT AGE FIFTEEN
1950–

I n the mid-1960s, fiction written for teenagers told only of carefree youth, sports heroes, and young love. Then came publication of Susan Hinton's *The Outsiders* in 1967. This novel broke the mold for young-adult fiction. The sensitive account of real-life teenagers with serious problems became an instant success. *The Outsiders* and its young author changed the way in which other authors wrote about young adults.

Reading and writing always had been important to Susan Hinton. Her earliest childhood memories were of reading everything—from children's books to food labels. And from a young age, she began writing about everything that interested her. Susan's favorite grade-school subjects were cowboys and horses. When she was young, Susan wanted to work on a cattle ranch. In Tulsa, Oklahoma, during the 1950s, ranching was a career many children (most often boys) wanted to pursue. Susan was shy, and she felt more comfortable with boys than girls. She liked boys' action-oriented activities more than the typical pursuits of girls.

At Tulsa's Will Rogers High School, Susan considered herself an outsider. She had friends among both the wealthier high-school students, called "socs" (for socials), and the poorer "greasers." She felt that she fit into neither group. Instead, she observed the two groups from a distance. She was outraged by the unfair, and sometimes dangerous, games they played against each other.

Susan found most fiction for teenagers unreal and boring. Real-life problems and violence were never portrayed in young-adult literature. Yet some of Susan's friends were getting beaten up, and even murdered, because of disagreements between socs and greasers. Susan wanted to write about her real life. It was so different from the unreal and always happy families that were depicted on television and in popular fiction.

By the time she was a high-school junior, Susan had her own serious problems. Her father was dying of cancer. With her mother and younger sister away at the hospital, Susan found writing was an outlet to ease her sadness. Susan began writing *The Outsiders* during this difficult time. It took Susan eighteen months to complete *The Outsiders* and have it accepted by a publisher. Many young authors write fiction, and some complete entire novels. But very few teenagers have the extraordinary talent and luck to get their work published nationally.

Since *The Outsiders* was written from a boy's viewpoint, Susan listed her name as S. E. Hinton. That way, she prevented potential male readers from thinking, "What can a girl know about a boy's life?"

The book was an instant success. Young readers discovered a writer who understood what it was like to be a teenager. Book critics applauded the author's honesty. Only some adults worried that a setting where kids lived by their own rules encouraged lawlessness and gangs.

Millions of copies of *The Outsiders* were sold in its first year of publication. The book's success enabled Susan to attend and eventually graduate from the University of Tulsa. However, Susan was overwhelmed by her sudden fame. For several years, she had difficulty even writing a letter. Through four years of college, Susan produced just one short story, entitled "Rumble Fish." Discouraged by her "writer's block," she changed her major from journalism to education to take a break from trying to write.

Then Susan's college friend and future husband, David Inhofe, encouraged her to write again. Working at a steady pace of two pages a day, Susan slowly completed her second novel, *That Was Then, This Is Now*, when she was twenty-three years old. Susan's other four books, *Rumble Fish, Tex, Taming the Star Runner,* and *Big David, Little David,* came after long periods without writing.

By her own admission, Susan is a "quiet person, the kind who takes her time about things." She almost flunked creative writing in high school because she "couldn't spell and write under pressure." Meanwhile, her books continue to be widely read as young-adult classics.

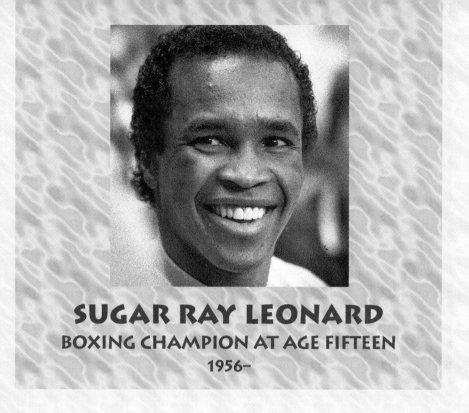

SUGAR RAY LEONARD
BOXING CHAMPION AT AGE FIFTEEN
1956–

Fourteen-year-old Ray Leonard followed his older brother into the recreation center near their home. The coach chuckled at the shy, skinny boy who wanted to box. But the coach quickly discovered what the world would soon learn. Ray was a natural-born boxer. Within two years, the teenager won the National Golden Gloves lightweight championship and the American Athletic Union junior boxing championship. Along the way, he defeated boxers five and ten years his senior.

Ray Leonard was born in Wilmington, North Carolina, the fifth of seven children in the working-class Leonard family. Getha Leonard named her baby Ray Charles after the famous rhythm-and-blues singer. She hoped that the name would inspire her son to become a famous singer. The family was struggling and needed some luck just to make ends meet.

When Ray was four, the Leonards moved to Washington, D.C., seeking a better life. Seven years later, the family moved to a nearby suburb in Maryland. Money problems continued to hamper the Leonards. One day, Ray stayed home from a school field trip because his parents could not spare the money to pay his way. At times, Ray and his siblings went without school lunches because they were too expensive.

Ray felt he was not as good as other children at school because his family was poor. He was normally a quiet youngster who never got into trouble. As Ray grew older, he became more of a loner. He spent most of his free time reading comic books at home. He also sang in the church choir. Ray liked singing; it was the one activity that made him feel he was worth something. Then he discovered boxing.

When Ray was fourteen, a recreation center opened near his home. His brother, Roger, enrolled in the center's boxing program. At first, Ray had little interest in fighting. Then Roger encouraged him to take a boxing lesson.

To everyone's surprise, Ray took to boxing as if he had been fighting for years. He learned each new step and technique after a single lesson. Ray had natural speed, style, and coordination. Within three months, coach Dave Jacobs remembers, "The scrawny neighborhood kid had something special. And his dedication—it was something you seldom find anymore."

Ray was a different person when he boxed. He was sure of himself. He felt happy and full of life. He knew he was a good boxer, but he also understood that he had a lot of hard work ahead of him. Every day after school, Ray raced to the center to practice. Before school, he jogged to build up speed and strength. Ray decided that boxing was his ticket out of the ghetto. He told his mother, "Mama, I'm puttin' the singin' into swingin'," and he left the choir for boxing.

In his first year as an amateur boxer, Ray won one match after another. When Ray beat the best amateur boxer in the area, Dave Jacobs decided Ray should enter national tournaments. Now Ray set his sights on the top, too. He wanted to represent the United States at the 1972 Olympics. But he was too young and weighed too little to meet Olympic standards. After watching Ray box, however, the Olympic tryout coach assured Jacobs, "That kid of yours is sweeter than sugar." From then on, Ray Charles Leonard was called "Sugar Ray."

With the 1972 Olympics out of the question, Ray had time to perfect his skills before the 1976 Olympic games in Montreal. In 1973, Ray won the National Golden Gloves championship in the 132-pound class, his first non-junior national title. In the next few years, he piled up one boxing title after another. By 1976, Ray went to the Olympics with a sparkling overall record of 139–5. He had won matches in almost every national and international amateur competition.

Ray took the world by storm at the Olympics. His gold-medal performance was only part of his appeal. He charmed audiences and television viewers with his quiet, sincere personality and good looks. People who knew nothing about boxing fell in love with Sugar Ray Leonard.

After the Olympics, Ray became a professional boxer. In the pro ring, he was equally unbeatable. He won titles in five different weight classes and retired in 1991 as one of the greatest boxing champions in the world.

Throughout his successful career, Ray never forgot his family and community. His fights earned him millions of dollars. With this money, he founded a corporation to assist his parents, brothers, and sisters with money and jobs. He helped poor children by supervising boxing teams and lending his name to worthwhile organizations, such as the American Library Association and National Safety Belt Council. The poor youth from North Carolina always remembered those who helped him reach boxing fame.

THE LITTLE ROCK NINE

If my Central High School experience taught me one lesson, it is that we are not separate. The effort to separate ourselves whether by race, creed, color, religion, or status is as costly to the separator as to those who would be separated.

— Melba Pattillo Beals

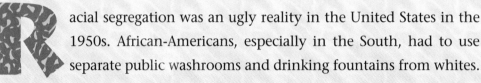acial segregation was an ugly reality in the United States in the 1950s. African-Americans, especially in the South, had to use separate public washrooms and drinking fountains from whites. They sat in bus seats designated "colored," if they found seats at all. They were banned from restaurants, stores, and theaters in white neighborhoods. At its worst, white racial hatred of blacks led to beatings, lynchings, and the burning of homes and businesses.

In many communities, laws forbade black children to attend the same schools as white children. Black public schools received less money than white schools, and the buildings were poorly maintained. Black children used hand-me-down books with the names of the white children who had already discarded them scribbled inside.

In 1954, the Supreme Court declared that separate schools for different races were unconstitutional. In the *Brown v. Board of Education of Topeka* case, the Court ruled that segregated schools denied African-American children the right to equal education. The Court ordered an end to school segregation.

Many whites resisted the teaching of black and white children together. Many school districts simply ignored the ruling of the Supreme Court. Others held meeting after meeting, trying to stall integration.

Civil rights groups battled in court to integrate one school district at a time. A landmark showdown came in Little Rock, Arkansas. In 1957, after three years of meetings, Little Rock schools finally agreed to allow nine African-American students to attend Central High School.

Ernest Green, Melba Pattillo, Minniejean Brown, Elizabeth Eckford, Thelma Mothershed, Gloria Ray, Carlotta Walls, Terrence Roberts, and Jefferson Thomas were chosen from a pool of students who wanted to integrate the schools. Each knew their fight might be unpleasant. But their strong beliefs in equality and justice pushed aside any doubts. "I never expected it to be life-threatening, which it was initially," recalled Ernest Green.

On the first day of school, Arkansas governor Orval Faubus ordered state National Guard troops to surround the school and allow only white students inside. Elizabeth Eckford failed to receive a message about where and when to meet the other eight black students before school, so she arrived at Central High alone. When she tried to pass through the troops' raised bayonets, Elizabeth was turned away. Angry crowds outside the school surrounded her, yelling, "Lynch her! Lynch her!"

Somehow, Elizabeth managed to escape unharmed. For the next three weeks, the group that became known as the "Little Rock Nine" stayed home. Then a federal court judge ordered Governor Faubus to withdraw the National Guard and open the school to the African-American students.

The following day all nine students slipped into school through a side door. Outside, however, the racist rage continued to grip the city. Angry protesters at the school attacked news reporters, both white and black. Many parents kept their children at home because they objected to the black students in school. Television news reported everything. The nation watched in horror.

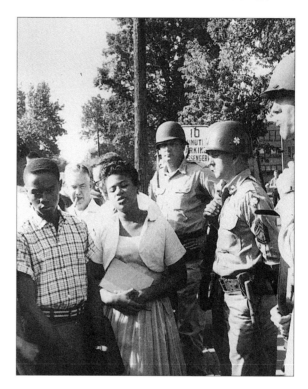

That night, President Dwight Eisenhower sent one thousand air force troops, jeeps, and helicopters to Little Rock. The next morning, armed guards escorted the African-American students into school. Guards followed each of the nine students to their classes and escorted them home. The students were never left alone.

After a few weeks, white students who opposed integration began returning to school. By November, the air force troops withdrew, and National Guard troops remained. But the threat to the Little Rock Nine never ended. Many white students attempted to drive the black students away with physical and verbal abuse.

Melba Pattillo later wrote a book about her experiences, titled *Warriors Don't Cry*. In it, she recalled, "While most teenage girls were listening to Buddy Holly's 'Peggy Sue,' watching Elvis gyrate, and collecting crinoline slips, I was escaping the hanging rope of a lynch mob, dodging lighted sticks of dynamite, and washing away burning acid sprayed into my eyes."

Teachers and administrators offered little help. Guards rarely stopped the pushing, shoving, or insults. Many black adults questioned why these stubborn black kids were making life harder for themselves and their community. The Little Rock Nine were isolated. Their only support came from their families and each other.

By Christmas, Minniejean Brown's nerves were frayed from the constant abuse. She was in line at the cafeteria one day when she finally snapped. A boy called her a name, and she dumped a bowl of chili on his head. The cafeteria workers, who were African-American, applauded. But the school board met and expelled Minnie from school. White students passed notes that read, "One down, eight to go."

The remaining eight teens, however, endured the entire school year. On May 27, 1958, Ernest Green (the only senior of the Nine) received his diploma. He was the first black student to graduate from Central High School in Little Rock. In a crowd of thousands, Ernest and his eight relatives were the only African-Americans to attend the graduation ceremony.

The next summer, Governor Faubus appealed to the courts to stop black students from attending Central High. At first, he succeeded in gaining a three-year delay. But a higher court reversed the ruling. Faubus responded by closing all Little Rock high schools. This enraged many white residents, who turned their anger toward the seven black students and their families. They were flooded with death threats.

As unrest increased, black civil rights leaders feared for the lives of the remaining seven students. They arranged for the students to move to different communities around the nation, where they lived with other families and graduated from high school.

Two years later, Central High was forced to admit two black students. Arkansas inched toward more equal education, as did other southern states. Brave African-Americans throughout the South broke racial barriers in many elementary schools, high schools, and colleges.

The Little Rock standoff remains one of the most dramatic battles in the struggle for civil rights. Nine brave teenagers enraged a hateful government, moved a president to act, and brought an entire nation into the civil rights debate.

*— Eight of the Little Rock Nine students on their way to court
to testify about their attempts to attend Central High School —*

WAYNE GRETZKY
EXTRAORDINARY HOCKEY PLAYER AT AGE TEN
1961–

Wayne Gretzky began playing hockey at the age of three in Brantford, Ontario, a town southwest of Toronto. Wayne's father, Walter, was a telephone technician who loved watching his son imitate famous hockey players by sliding across the living-room floor. To encourage the young skater, Walter flooded the backyard until it froze into an ice rink.

Walter taught Wayne how to skate. When he saw Wayne's agility on skates, Walter trained the boy in handling a hockey stick, passing a puck, and shooting goals. Walter invented drills for his son, such as skating through obstacle courses and hopping over sticks. Wayne recovered pucks his father shot off the rink sideboards. Walter taught Wayne to "go where the puck's going, not where it's been."

When Wayne was six, he joined a local hockey team of ten-year-olds. That season he scored one goal. Over the next two years, however, Wayne established a reputation for scoring against boys four and six years older than himself. His special skill at controlling the puck allowed him to score, or to pass the puck for someone else to score.

By his tenth birthday, Wayne averaged an outstanding four goals per game. He received a special trophy from his childhood hockey idol, Gordie Howe, for his incredible performance. Media and the general public noticed this rising star. Even before he was a teenager, Wayne was giving interviews and signing autographs.

Wayne's enthusiasm for hockey increased as he grew older. He gave up many activities other boys his age enjoy to pursue a hockey career. At fourteen, he left home to play in a junior league, where the average player was two years older than he was. Still, Wayne was the top scorer for the team, and he acquired his nickname, "The Great Gretzky."

Wayne feared that if he stayed within the junior league, his skills would decline. He jumped at the chance to sign a four-year, $875,000 contract with the World Hockey Association's Indianapolis Racers. There, he played with some men who were old enough to be his father! The high-school senior became the youngest member of a U.S. professional sports team.

After Wayne had played just eight games, the Racers' team owner decided he needed money. He sold Wayne's contract to the Edmonton Oilers of the National Hockey League (NHL). Wayne moved closer to home, lived with an Edmonton family, and enrolled in high school to earn a diploma. Meanwhile, his career took off. In his rookie season, he became the youngest player in NHL history to score more than fifty goals. It wasn't long before fans all over Canada and the United States realized that Wayne Gretzky was the greatest hockey player alive.

After being traded to the Los Angeles Kings in 1988, Wayne's reputation as a sports legend was guaranteed. He is now the all-time leader in goals and points in NHL history. The Great Gretzky has collected numerous most valuable player awards, as well as honors for his charitable work off the ice.

Perhaps the most amazing thing about Wayne Gretzky is how polite and gentle he is *on* the ice. Many hockey players rely on fighting and rough play to gain an advantage over opponents. Wayne Gretzky is tough and will not back down. But he relies on his brains, not his fists, to prove himself on the ice. Wayne is known for his pinpoint shooting, his blinding skating speed, and his astonishing passing abilities. It should not come as a shock that he is the greatest in the sport. He's been at it since he was three years old!

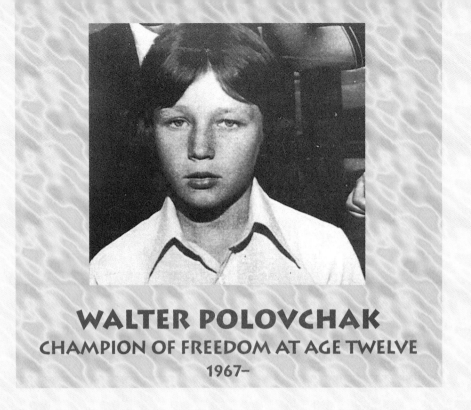

WALTER POLOVCHAK
CHAMPION OF FREEDOM AT AGE TWELVE
1967–

The twelve-year-old boy told police: "I don't want to go back with my parents [to the Soviet Union] because I like this country. I can go to church without people following me around." Walter Polovchak vowed to stay in the United States at all costs. Over the next six years, Walter bravely battled his parents, the United States courts, and the mighty Soviet government to remain in a country where he could be free.

The Polovchak family moved to the United States in 1980. They had emigrated from Sambir, a small city in the western Ukraine area of the Soviet Union. They came to the United States seeking a better life. But when the Polovchaks decided they were happier in the Ukraine, their twelve-year-old son announced he preferred America. Walter Polovchak became the focus of an international controversy.

Life in the Ukraine had been difficult for the Polovchaks. Michael and Anna Polovchak worked eight hours almost every day of the week. Their wages barely kept the family fed, and they both had little time to spend with their three children. Little Walter, his brother, and sister were lucky to be raised by their grandmother, whose home they shared. Their house did not have running water or an indoor bathroom. A garden, fruit orchard, and some animals provided food that was usually unavailable in Soviet stores.

When Walter's grandmother died, he felt he lost the only parent he really knew. He was ready for change when his father announced that the family was moving to the United States in hopes of finding a more comfortable life.

In January 1980, Walter felt both hope and fear as his family arrived in New York City. He watched brightly lit runways and scurrying workers unloading baggage from airplanes. Already America was more exciting than he had dreamed. At that moment, Walter decided he never would return to the Ukraine. In the days ahead, he continually was amazed at the number of choices citizens had in America. Even dogs and cats had their own aisle of food in the supermarket!

The family settled in Chicago, but Walter's father did not find the United States so wonderful. Michael Polovchak felt uncomfortable in the foreign surroundings, where everyone spoke an unfamiliar language. He wanted to leave immediately and return alone to the Ukraine. But Soviet authorities ordered him to bring back everyone on his passport. His daughter, Natalie, had her own passport, so she could stay in the United States. But Anna, Mikey, and Walter shared Michael's passport, so by law they had to return if Michael did.

The family split when Natalie moved into a cousin's apartment. Since she was nearly eighteen, her parents said she could make up her own mind about staying in the United States. But soon enough twelve-year-old Walter packed his bags and moved to the cousin's house, too.

On July 18, 1980, Walter's nightmare deepened. Chicago police arrested him while he was fixing his bicycle in his cousin's yard. Walter's father had called the police and reported him as a runaway. Natalie ran from the house just as patrolmen put her brother in the back seat of a squad car.

Natalie made contact with a Ukrainian-American lawyer. The lawyer rushed to the police station. He argued with the police, attempting to keep officers from returning Walter to his angry father. Everyone feared that Michael would waste no time getting his son on a plane to the Soviet Union.

The police questioned Walter all day. With his limited English, Walter explained again and again that he had run away from his parents because he wanted to stay in the United States. By the next day, newspapers around the country carried the story of the boy who ran away from his parents so he could live in freedom. Soviet representatives read the story, too. They pressured Michael to return with his entire family. The Soviets refused to be embarrassed by a twelve-year-old boy.

Walter's lawyer requested an emergency court hearing to place Walter where he would be safe from the long arm of Soviet authority. First, a judge made Walter and Natalie wards of the state of Illinois. Then, he allowed the children to go home with their American relatives. Walter was told to stay under guard for safekeeping. His father, who understood little of what had happened, was furious that this strange government had taken his children from him.

A group of lawyers decided to help Michael and Anna get their son back. For six years, Walter and Natalie were marched in and out of court for an endless series of hearings. Walter's lawyers contended he was old enough to understand the differences between a free and a restricted society. He should be allowed to decide for himself where he would live. His parents' lawyers claimed that a boy his age should be with his parents, no matter where the family lived.

As the case dragged on, Walter and Natalie tried to lead normal lives.

Walter went to school, learned English, played soccer, and began to make friends. Occasionally he and his sister had difficult visits with their parents. Most of the time, Michael Polovchak yelled at his children and called them ugly names.

Eventually, the Polovchaks surprised everyone by taking their youngest son, Mikey, and returning to the Ukraine. They told no one they were leaving. They never said good-bye to their older children.

Five days after Walter Polovchak turned eighteen in October 1985, he flew to Washington, D.C. At a special ceremony, he was sworn in as a citizen of the United States. Surrounded by his American friends and family, the courageous boy said: "I'm not sure yet about my future career, but I am sure of one thing: I pledge here and now that I will be the best American I can be."

— *Eighteen-year-old Walter Polovchak became a U.S. citizen in 1985.* —

MIDORI
OUTSTANDING VIOLINIST AT AGE EIGHT
1971–

A mature attitude paired with a brilliant musical talent is Midori's formula for worldwide success. This unique combination made her debut at the Tanglewood Music Festival unforgettable. People still talk about the youngster's extraordinary debut.

The fourteen-year-old violinist was performing with Leonard Bernstein, the legendary conductor. In the middle of a complex violin concerto, a string on Midori's violin snapped. Her violin was unusable, and Maestro Bernstein stopped the orchestra. Midori kept her cool, turned to the first violinist, and borrowed his violin. Incredibly, a string quickly broke on *that* violin as well, and Midori had to use yet another instrument. Such a disaster might unnerve even an experienced soloist, but Midori kept her cool and finished the concerto. The response was a roaring ovation from the audience and raves from critics around the world.

Young Midori had always loved music. As a little girl in Osaka, Japan, Midori lived in a musical home. Her mother, Setsu Goto, was a concert violinist. Setsu's demanding practice schedule forced her to bring little Midori to the music studio. When Midori was just two years old, her mother was amazed to hear her child humming a complex concerto by Bach.

Midori soon began practicing on a child-sized violin. Her mother gave her music lessons and arranged private performances for family and friends. When Midori was nine years old, her mother recognized that her daughter possessed incredible musical talent. She took Midori to the United States to play at the Aspen Music Festival. After Midori performed flawlessly there, a famous music teacher named Dorothy DeLay accepted her as her student. This meant that Midori and her mother would have to move to New York City.

In New York, Midori had to learn a new language and an entirely new culture. At the same time, she maintained a busy schedule of music lessons and school. Gradually she made friends and learned to love New York City.

After her sensational Tanglewood debut, music fans eagerly waited for each of her concerts. In her early teens, Midori performed only a few times a year. She was attending the prestigious Juilliard School of Music, and she wanted to leave enough time for practice and study.

When she turned sixteen, Midori decided to leave Juilliard and become a full-time performer. The life of a professional violinist was everything Midori had hoped for. When she appeared onstage, audiences were enchanted by Midori's graceful, shy beauty. As she played, observers were enthralled with the lush and sophisticated sound she produced.

The adult Midori is perhaps the most famous female musician in the world. Her concerts are sold out around the world. She has received countless awards. But Midori is not just wrapped up in her career. She recently created the Midori Foundation. This agency provides lecture-demonstrations to teach children about music. Midori remembers how much she loved learning to make music as a child. Now, she is devoted to making the same beautiful experience possible for other young children.

EMMA GARCIA
COMMUNITY ORGANIZER AT AGE SIXTEEN
1972–

Every generation of adults claims that kids are wilder, care less about their community, or are more violent than kids "in our day." Adults tend to forget the neighborhood turf wars that went on in most cities in every generation. They overlook how kids naturally tease each other and argue in the streets, playgrounds, and alleys. The difference now, however, is that many more conflicts between young people turn deadly. Guns kill more teens than AIDS, cancer, and heart disease combined. Emma Garcia and several students at Oakland High School in California wanted to reverse that trend.

Emma came from a loving family, but one that struggled economically. Until Emma was four, her parents moved frequently in order to find work. In 1976, the family migrated from Baja, in Mexico, to the Oakland area.

Emma spoke only Spanish until she learned English in the first grade. As the oldest of four children, she became the family translator. Emma helped her parents prepare tax forms and other documents in English, a big responsibility for someone so young. The family proudly maintained their Mexican customs. But her parents always emphasized the importance of school and of contributing to the community, wherever they lived.

Emma and her brothers and sister often joined other children in the streets of their diverse Oakland neighborhood. They spent many evenings playing hide-and-seek in the dark. By the time Emma was nine, however, the neighborhood had changed. Several large companies had moved, leaving about twenty percent of the adults without jobs. Drug dealers entered the once-safe neighborhood. With the drug trade came violence and guns. Soon, Emma and her friends feared going out at night.

As a teenager, the effects of neighborhood violence affected Emma's school life. Emma was upset that her school never held dances or extracurricular activities that other teens enjoyed. Teachers feared drive-by shootings before and after school events. They worried that school functions were magnets for drug dealers. And a dangerous practice arose—shooting guns into the air at school dances.

Budget cuts further hurt local school districts. Some classes were eliminated, as were arts and sports programs. Poor neighborhoods like Emma's were hit hardest. Emma and her friends had nothing to keep themselves busy when they were not in class. Kids who were bored with schoolwork had no other activities that attracted them to school. The result was a sixty-percent dropout rate at Oakland High School. Drugs and violence overtook the school. Forty percent of the girls at the school got pregnant.

Emma set her goals higher than most of her classmates. She was a good student and the editor of the school newspaper. Her enthusiasm for learning earned her a place in a special school media program. She taught Sunday school and was involved in many church activities. "The activities and the good people I met gave me a strong sense of working for change in the community," she says.

But these successes couldn't erase Emma's sadness about what was happening to her friends. The murder rate for young people in Oakland was soaring, and several of Emma's friends were killed. After a record-breaking year of killings in her high school, sixteen-year-old Emma knew something had to be done.

So did the Oakland Unified School District. The school asked Deanne Calhoun (who worked for an injury-prevention group) to work with students in Emma's media program. Emma and seven classmates formed the core of what evolved into "Teens on Target," the first youth violence-prevention program in the United States.

Part of Emma's class produced a videotape. Meanwhile, Emma helped devise a questionnaire to ask other kids what they thought about violence in their neighborhoods. The survey brought an overwhelming response. Kids said they desperately wanted to talk. Mostly, they wanted to talk with other kids whom they trusted, not to adults.

Emma's class decided to organize a conference in the Bay Area as a forum to explore ideas further. Emma spent the summer before her senior year at the media center. She worked with local school and community organizations to brainstorm about what to include in the conference. The fall 1989 conference covered four areas of violence: family; gang and street; gun; and drug and alcohol.

More than two hundred kids from the San Francisco Bay Area attended the conference. They represented middle- and high-school students from a variety of ethnic and social backgrounds. Some were teens who had been arrested and attended as part of their parole agreements.

At the conference, the teenagers agreed that violence had taken over their neighborhoods, and that something must be done. They said that young people needed more information about the effects of guns and violence. They needed to learn how to resolve conflicts peacefully. Moreover, they wanted to talk with their peers about these issues, not with adults.

As a result of the conference, Emma Garcia took it upon herself to educate students. She received training from Youth Alive, a public health agency. With her teachers' permission, she gave presentations in junior-high and high-school classes three to four times over a three-week period. More than fifty similarly trained students joined Emma.

Teens on Target soon expanded to Los Angeles, explaining violence prevention to nearly a thousand kids a year. Adults in state and local agencies were surprised that kids like Emma had so many good ideas about such serious issues. In 1990, Emma attended a national conference for public health officials. She and Teens on Target brought the message that kids were dying from more serious threats than a lack of bicycle helmets. Her group gained much-needed attention from the public health workers.

In Oakland, Emma urged lawmakers to expand and enforce laws banning billboards advertising liquor and cigarettes near schools. She was angry that her classmates could get guns, liquor, and drugs near school, but had to take a bus to buy school supplies. Emma also appealed to voters in the 1995 election to set aside one percent of the state budget for youth issues.

Emma graduated from high school and college. But she stayed committed to Teens on Target and ending youth violence. Emma started as a Teens on Target rookie, then became a trainer, and then became program director. She coordinated school presentations and special projects for younger kids. She wrote a training manual for incoming Teens on Target role models and organized news conferences.

"The community has a lot to do with what individuals do with their lives, whether they become college students or drug dealers," Emma stresses. "It's important for young people to contribute to the community, and for the community to care about its young people. Kids have to speak out!"

SAMANTHA REED SMITH
AMBASSADOR FOR PEACE AT AGE TEN
1972–1985

The Cold War between the United States and the Soviet Union stretched from the late 1940s through the 1980s. Soviet and U.S. leaders criticized each other for promoting an arms race to see which country could stockpile the most powerful nuclear weapons. As the two nations maneuvered for power, millions of citizens worldwide felt helpless about the threat of war.

A ten-year-old girl named Samantha Reed Smith was so worried about nuclear war that she wrote a letter to Soviet leader Yuri V. Andropov. She asked him why he wanted to go to war. His answer and Samantha's resulting visit to the Soviet Union made people realize that individuals, even children, can take action and be heard.

Samantha lived in the small town of Manchester, Maine, with her parents, Jane and Arthur Smith, two cats, and a Chesapeake Bay retriever. Samantha belonged to the Girl Scouts and enjoyed swimming, other sports, animals, and rock music. Her friends and teachers considered her a thoughtful and caring girl, someone who valued good neighbors, friend-ship, and nature, above all else.

Samantha thought very often about world peace. Frequently, she saw television and news stories discussing how nuclear war would destroy the earth. After reading one of these stories, Samantha urged her mother to write to Yuri Andropov to find out why his country seemed to want war. Her mother suggested that Samantha should write the letter herself. Saman-tha wrote:

> *Dear Mr. Andropov,*
>
> *My name is Samantha Smith. I am ten years old. Congratula-tions on your new job. I have been worrying about Russia and the United States getting into a nuclear war. Are you going to vote to have a war or not? If you aren't please tell me how you are going to help to not have a war. This question you do not have to answer, but I would like to know why you want to conquer the world or at least our country. God made the world for us to live together in peace and not to fight.*
>
> *Sincerely,*
> *Samantha Smith*

For months, Samantha heard nothing. Then, just when she had almost forgotten about her letter, a journalist telephoned. He asked Samantha if she was the girl who had written a letter that was published in the Soviet newspaper, *Pravda*. The article in *Pravda* gave no hint whether Andropov would respond. However, it forgave the ten-year-old for misunderstanding what Andropov and the Soviets were like.

Samantha believed her question was important no matter what age she was, and she wanted an answer from Andropov. So she wrote to Ambas-sador Dobrynin, who represented the Soviet Union in Washington, D.C.

This letter brought a lengthy reply from Andropov, saying that Samantha was a "courageous and honest girl." In his letter, Andropov asserted, "We in the Soviet Union are trying to do everything so that there will not be war between our countries." He also invited Samantha and her family to visit the Soviet Union to see for herself that "in the Soviet Union everyone is for peace and friendship among peoples."

News of Samantha's letter was broadcast around the globe, including the Soviet Union. Soviets wanted to know more about the brave girl who dared write to the premier of the Soviet Union at a time when United States-Soviet relations were shaky.

On July 7, 1983, Samantha and her parents departed on a two-week trip to the Soviet Union. They were accompanied by reporters and photographers. Samantha went sightseeing, met important government officials (although not Andropov), and stayed at Pioneer Camp. The camp was for the most talented Soviet children. They went there for special training based on communist teachings. Everywhere she went, Samantha charmed the Soviets with her enthusiastic manner and bright smile.

When Samantha returned home, she continued her peace mission. She accepted speaking engagements and television interviews to "tell grownups the truth about the Soviet people" and their desire "to live in friendship with all peoples." Samantha's father helped her write a book, *Samantha Smith: A Journey to the Soviet Union,* so that she could share her travel experiences with other children. In her book, she wrote:

> *If we could be friends by just getting to know each other*
> *better, then what are our countries really arguing about?*
> *Nothing could be more important than not having a war*
> *if war would kill everything.*

Five months after the Soviet visit, Samantha went to Japan as the keynote speaker for the Children's International Symposium. At home,

Samantha hosted a ninety-minute television show in which she interviewed U.S. presidential candidates. After several talk-show appearances, Samantha accepted an offer to act on television. She appeared in an episode of "Charles in Charge" and began filming "Lime Street" in London.

The thirteen-year-old girl's life was blossoming when it ended suddenly and tragically. Traveling from London to the United States, Samantha and her father died in a plane crash. More than a thousand mourners crowded into the church to mourn Samantha's death. President Ronald Reagan and the new Soviet leader, Mikhail Gorbachev, sent letters of condolence to Samantha's mother. The Soviet Union named a flower, a star, and a children's center after Samantha to keep alive the memory of her goodwill. Back home in Maine , a statue of Samantha was erected. It shows her with a dove (a symbol of peace) and a bear (a Soviet symbol).

Samantha's mother, Jane Smith, later established the Samantha Smith Foundation. The foundation continues to sponsor youth exchanges between the United States and countries that comprise the former Soviet Union. Jane Smith wants to help realize her daughter's vision of world peace.

— *The memorial statue of Samantha Smith that stands in Augusta, Maine* —

RYAN WHITE
CHAMPION OF AIDS PATIENTS' RIGHTS
AT AGE FOURTEEN
1972–1990

When Ryan White developed Acquired Immunodeficiency Syndrome (AIDS), few people knew much about the illness, except that it was something to fear. Ryan's struggle to live and be accepted led the nation to greater understanding about the disease and patients who suffer from it.

Ryan White was born and grew up in Kokomo, Indiana, where he lived with his younger sister, Andrea, and mother, Jeanne, after his parents divorced. He was born with hemophilia, a disorder that prevents a person's blood from clotting.

To keep him from bleeding, Ryan's mother would give him two or three injections of new blood each month. In the 1970s, nobody knew that some of the world's blood supply had been infected with AIDS. Like many other people, Ryan acquired the disease from a seemingly innocent blood transfusion.

Just after his thirteenth birthday, Ryan and his family learned he had AIDS. At the time, he felt pretty healthy. He maintained good grades at junior high school, had a girlfriend, and played baseball. Within a year, however, the first of many AIDS symptoms flared up and left him weak and sickly.

As he recovered, Ryan looked forward to going back to school. But his community panicked. Parents worried that their children could catch his disease by being in the same classroom with him. Frightened parents voiced their concerns to the school district. These people did not understand that AIDS cannot be transmitted through the air, through touch, or through saliva. The disease exists only in the blood. The only way for Ryan to infect others was if Ryan's blood came in contact with another child's open wound. Such an event was highly unlikely.

Despite these medical facts, many parents in Kokomo, Indiana, wanted Ryan White barred from public school. In 1985, Ryan's mother won a court battle to allow her son to attend school. Until the ruling, Ryan was forced to receive part of his seventh-grade education by telephone at home. "All I wanted was to go to school and fit in," said Ryan.

Newspapers reported the ruling and the hostile reaction from many Kokomo residents. Some parents kept their children home from school when Ryan returned to the eighth grade. Most students who came to school avoided any contact with Ryan. Many called him names.

Townspeople threw eggs at the Whites' car and slashed its tires. The windows of their house were broken, and someone even shot a bullet through the living-room window. After that much abuse, the Whites decided to move. By then, the entire nation knew of the family's problems due to constant media attention. Throughout the ordeal, Ryan never complained or became bitter.

The new school district in Cicero, Indiana, went out of its way to welcome Ryan. The superintendent held information sessions with students and their parents to give them facts about AIDS. By the time Ryan started school, he was generally accepted.

As Ryan's story became better known, he received many requests to appear in public. Even though he craved a normal life, he welcomed opportunities to help other children with AIDS. The teenager appeared on television talk shows and at benefits, and he granted magazine interviews. He also addressed a White House hearing about AIDS. With a message of hope and faith, Ryan informed the public about what it was like to have AIDS. He never presented himself as a sick person. Instead, he emphasized how he was a student with the same desires and concerns as any other.

Ryan's fight with the Kokomo community aroused the support of several celebrities. Stars such as Greg Louganis, Elton John, and Michael Jackson went out of their way to befriend Ryan and appear with him in public. They wanted to dispel the fear that someone could get AIDS by touching or being in the same room with a person who has AIDS. Well-known people sent Ryan photos and gifts to help keep up his spirits. Some even invited his family on vacations they otherwise could not have afforded due to mounting medical bills.

On April 8, 1990, Ryan White died in an Indianapolis hospital. His funeral brought together about 1,500 people—friends, family, and celebrities alike. They came to honor the courageous spokesperson for young people with AIDS. Because of what Ryan went through and how he kept his enthusiasm for life, Ryan opened doors of hope for other children with AIDS.

BETHANY WAIT
HERO DURING HURRICANE ELENA
AT AGE TWELVE
1973–1991

ethany Wait first became interested in amateur radio (also called "ham radio") when she was seven. Her father and mother talked to friends around the world on radio equipment in their home. Bethany often listened and watched as they sent messages over the wires to ham buddies. She had many questions. When she asked, "Can I do that?" her father was thrilled.

For the next six months, Bethany's father taught her how to operate an amateur radio. Bethany also learned Morse code, the international system of sounds that represent letters and numbers. When she was eight, she passed the beginner's test for her novice license from the Federal Communications Commission (FCC), a United States regulating agency. Bethany had earned the right to send codes from her radio station under the code number KA4WRJ.

Bethany loved her new hobby. She was excited to reach people in other countries and understand their code. Her first two contacts were with ham-radio operators in Sweden and Germany. The German man was a veterinarian who sent her a letter and pictures of his home and dogs. Still, Bethany wanted to talk to people without a code. That meant more studying to get her license for the next level of ham operation. When Bethany passed the technician exam, she received a handheld radio that enabled her to send and receive messages wherever she went. People commented about how unusual it was to see a child clutch a doll in one hand while talking into a hand radio in the other.

Bethany continued studying and upgrading her radio license. Higher-level licenses required her to learn technical theory and greater understanding of Morse code. But Bethany was determined to reach the top. By the time she was twelve, Bethany passed exams for the highest level of FCC license. She became the youngest Amateur Extra Class licensee in the United States.

The proud seventh-grader wanted to serve the community with her radio skills. Shortly after receiving her license, Bethany joined the Amateur Radio Emergency Service. Bethany and the other adults met twice a week and organized monthly drills. Members practiced setting up emergency radio networks in case normal communications (such as telephone, radio, or television) were interrupted. In an emergency, amateur radio operators relay vital information until regular communications are restored.

Late in the summer of 1985, Hurricane Elena ripped across central Florida. As the hurricane approached Bethany's hometown of Jacksonville, the Red Cross called on her radio group for assistance. The ham operators rushed to their emergency stations. Twelve-year-old Bethany fought the driving rain to reach her local high school. She set up her radio as families crowded into the school to escape the hurricane's floodwaters.

Bethany knew everyone would need food and bedding. She broadcast urgent messages trying to locate the supplies. Over her radio, she received reports of people stranded by the storm. Many needed supplies, or a way to reach safety. Bethany stayed on the radio for hours and arranged for these people to be evacuated.

The hurricane lasted for three days, and Bethany was at her radio virtually the entire time. Her back ached from sitting so long, and her eyes hurt from lack of sleep. But she stayed at her station until power was restored and communication lines opened. For more than three days, Bethany was her community's link to the world. Florida's governor sent Bethany a letter thanking her for her work.

A year later, Bethany provided the same kind of emergency service when a major forest fire raged in Florida. Bethany's father, other radio operators, and police carrying walkie-talkies patrolled the area. Bethany's job was to staff her home radio station. Those on patrol called information in to Bethany. In turn, the thirteen-year-old relayed news to volunteer firefighters so they could contain the fire.

Bethany amazed members of the emergency team with her ability to handle the radio during the crisis. She was able to concentrate for a long time and under high stress. And she accurately relayed complex, crucial messages. She was a child doing an adult's job—and doing it well.

Tragically, Bethany Wait died in a car crash on her eighteenth birthday. But her memory will live on in the hearts of those people whose lives she saved with her home radio station.

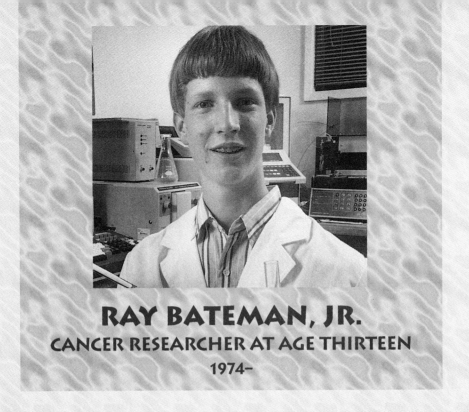

RAY BATEMAN, JR.
CANCER RESEARCHER AT AGE THIRTEEN
1974–

Dr. Glenn Tisman, a cancer specialist, knew his young neighbor, Ray Bateman, Jr., had an unusual mind. The boy was able to assemble a complex stereo system after two experts had bungled the job. But Tisman had no idea at the time that twelve-year-old Ray had the ability to become his partner in advanced cancer research.

Ray was a normal, playful child. Growing up in Huntington Beach, California, he enjoyed his share of horror movies, pizza, and rock music. Looking back, his parents remembered hints of their son's talent for solving mechanical problems. At age four, Ray surprised his mother by fixing a broken vacuum cleaner. He took it apart and put it together again. When he was ten, he speedily constructed the family color television from a kit.

Ray surprised his teachers, too. At first, the youngster did poorly in school. He had a hard time getting along with classmates. Ray figured he was just dumb. A few tests from a psychologist proved the opposite. Ray scored unusually high in math. His teachers realized that Ray was not a poor student, but that he was bored with regular classwork.

When Ray was ten, he convinced his parents to buy him a computer. Then, a whole new world opened. In a short time, Ray was able to do amazing things with the computer. Ray shared his enthusiasm for computers with Dr. Tisman, who used a computer for his research. The two discussed computers and medicine frequently. Remarkably, Ray understood the biology and chemistry involved in Dr. Tisman's medical research without any prior instruction. "It's really strange," Ray said. "I know a lot, but I have no idea how I got to know it."

One day, Ray asked Dr. Tisman for ideas for his school science project. The doctor thought for a while, and then he remembered that he had received a complex new machine for testing blood. The machine had arrived unassembled, and the manual explaining how to assemble it was a thousand pages long. Dr. Tisman offered Ray a chance to put the machine together. Ray read the complex manual and returned in a week to set up the six-foot-long computer system.

Ray then worked with Dr. Tisman after school and during school holidays. He helped conduct research with the equipment and keep it in working order. The purpose of the research was to test the effectiveness of mixing an old cancer drug with certain vitamins. Ray analyzed patient test results by computer, while Dr. Tisman handled all patient contact. Together, they came up with solid research that helped advance cancer treatment.

In 1988, fourteen-year-old Ray Bateman went with Dr. Tisman to a meeting of the American Federation for Clinical Research, where Ray presented their initial research findings. He was probably the youngest researcher to present to the group. Using terminology beyond the grasp of most kids his age, Ray told the scientists how the new drug mixture caused fewer and milder side effects for cancer patients.

A year later, Ray returned to update the federation on his and Dr. Tisman's research. By then, word had spread of the young researcher. He became renowned for his dedication to finding cures for sick patients. The International Platform Association, a group of famous people who present speeches, invited Ray to be its first young speaker. Stories about Ray appeared in hundreds of newspapers around the world and in several magazines. He appeared on television newscasts and talk shows. One talk show brought his family to Italy, where Ray discussed science with a European audience.

Back home, Ray tried to lead a normal life. His hobbies expanded to snow and water skiing and various forms of music—that is, when he had time. Ray's parents enrolled him in a private college preparatory school that offered challenging coursework. An adviser there compared Ray's level of intelligence to that of Albert Einstein, perhaps the most famous scientist of the century.

Even though he lived at school, Ray continued to spend most free hours working with Dr. Tisman. The two began studying the effects of vitamins on babies inside the womb. However, Ray's main interest remained cancer treatment, and he continues his research and education today.

SAVION GLOVER
TAP DANCE STAR AT AGE TWELVE
1974–

Adults in the arts are amazed when children perform near the level of adults. When Savion Glover came along, he astonished dancers and audiences alike. Here was a kid who was undoubtedly better than most of the adults in his field.

Twelve-year-old Savion Glover burst on the dance scene as the star of the Broadway show *The Tap Dance Kid*. Three years later, Savion starred in the 1989 show *Black and Blue*, giving a performance for which the *New York Times* proclaimed him a "tap dance master."

Throughout his teen years, Savion spent countless hours hanging out with the world's greatest living tap dancers. He took lessons from Sammy Davis, Jr., Jimmy Slyde, Honi Coles—all legends in the world of tap. Savion studied closely with legendary tapmaster Henry Le Tang, but his greatest influence was Gregory Hines.

Hines, himself, had been a young tap star, along with his brother, Maurice. When Hines and Savion co-starred in the 1988 film, *Tap*, the two dancers formed a teacher-student relationship that continues to this day. To Hines's amazement, the student regularly outperformed the teacher. When the two dancers starred together in *Jelly's Last Jam* on Broadway in 1992, every show featured an improvisation showdown between the two master dancers. Hines remembers, "It's frightening to be in a dance challenge with Savion. Winning was never in question."

Performing (and even competing) onstage with dancing legends like Gregory Hines would make most kids nervous. But Savion claims he has only been nervous twice in his performing life: "When I did my first performance in *The Tap Dance Kid*; and once when Gregory called me on stage at the Apollo Theater to dance with him."

Yvette Glover named her son "Savion" as a variation of "saviour" because she was convinced he was blessed by God from the day he was born. As a toddler, Savion was into rhythm. He banged out rhythms on any objects he touched around the house. Yvette remembers, "He would tap in the bathroom. When he walked to school, he tapped." His mother tried to enroll Savion in a drumming class at age four, but the teacher wouldn't take the child. The teacher said Savion was far too advanced to take class with the other students.

Savion's destiny on Broadway was soon paved. He began studying dance in New York City when he was seven years old. But Savion Glover was a restless teenager. He was not satisfied with doing things the way everyone else did. He began integrating his love of basketball and rap music into his tap performances. He developed a style that respected traditional tap, but was still as original as anyone could remember.

Today Savion Glover is committed to exploring the African rhythms in tap. In 1995, he choreographed and starred in a tap dance show called *Bring in Da Noise, Bring in Da Funk* at the Public Theater in New York City. The show drew rave reviews from critics, who said that Savion was bringing tap in to a new era of popularity.

Whenever Savion travels and performs in other cities, he holds special classes to teach kids about tap. He wants to keep the rich, African-American tap dance heritage alive. When he teaches, he doesn't want kids just to memorize old-fashioned dance steps.

He wants to see people express themselves from the heart. He says to students, "I wanna see what you got. . . . The complete expression of you in the moment. No restrictions. How you feel. How you hear the rhythms."

MODERN STARS OF TELEVISION, MUSIC, AND FILM

Child stars can be wealthy, and they often live luxurious lives. But some young stars pay dearly for their lives of fame. With television cameras seeking them out wherever they go, it's hard for today's stars to have any sort of private lives. Young performers endure long hours of practice and rehearsal, and they are forced to be as responsible as adults long before they are ready. Some young celebrities, however, have loving and supportive families who help them through these intense years.

— Brandy —

Brandy Norwood is a worldwide recording star who still is close to her family and lives a down-to-earth life. Brandy has loved entertaining crowds for as long as she can remember. Her first public singing performance was not in a packed stadium, but in a church. Under the direction of her father, Brandy amazed church members with her captivating voice at age four.

Born in McComb, Mississippi, Brandy's family moved to California when she was young. Brandy quickly moved from singing in the church choir to directing her own choir and organizing talent shows.

When she was eleven years old, she hit the big time when she landed a role in the sitcom "Thea." The program was soon cancelled. But by then, Brandy had signed a recording contract with Atlantic Records. Her debut album, *Brandy*, went platinum and skyrocketed her to fame. Today Brandy is one of the hottest singers in the world.

Like Brandy, **Tevin Campbell** first found singing success in a church choir. Until he was eleven years old, most of Tevin's singing was done in churches in his hometown, Waxahachie, Texas. That was where Menny Medina, an executive at Warner Records, discovered the young talent. Tevin first found a national audience through his performances on albums with the famous musicians, Quincy

— *Tevin Campbell* —

Jones and Prince. By the time he was fifteen, Tevin had two hit solo albums, and he was a teenage heartthrob to thousands of fans.

Today, record companies search for talented young performers like Tevin and Brandy. The companies sign them up, groom them to be stars, and launch their careers. But long before today's generation of teen stars were born, **Stevie Wonder** debuted in the 1950s as the first rhythm-and-blues child sensation. Stevie was born blind, but he developed a remarkable sense of hearing. Throughout his childhood in Detroit, Michigan, Stevie loved to sing and to play different instruments. By age nine, Motown Records president Berry Gordy had discovered Stevie's talent. Gordie billed the new star as "Little Stevie Wonder" when he first broke

— *Stevie Wonder* —

into the big time. Now, some thirty years later, Stevie Wonder remains one of the greatest music talents in the country. Equally superb as singer, musician, and composer, Stevie is truly a wonder.

A decade after Little Stevie Wonder's debut, another African-American music sensation swept the nation. **The Jackson Five** burst on the scene in 1969.

The Jacksons were a working-class family from Gary, Indiana. Joe Jackson worked in the steel mills, and even though it was difficult to put food on the table, he scraped together money to buy guitars and drums for his talented children. After years of winning trophies at local talent shows, the five Jackson brothers won a major amateur contest at the Apollo Theater in New York City.

Jackie, Jermaine, Marlon, Tito, and Michael Jackson caught the eye of Berry Gordy. The Jackson family moved to California, and Gordy molded the Jackson Five into an exciting rhythm-and-blues group. Then

— *The Jackson Five* —

he launched the group into the national spotlight. In 1970, their first three singles hit the charts, each selling more than a million copies.

The Jacksons then went on the road and sold out concerts wherever they played. Their music bridged the gap between African-American and white audiences. Hysterical teens screamed at the sight of them, especially for Michael. His lightning-quick dance moves and angelic voice had made him the group's standout star.

The Jackson Five eventually faded, but **Michael Jackson**'s career has become legend. His first solo album came out when he was thirteen years old. In 1984, he captured the imagination of the world when he displayed his incredible "moonwalk" dancing on a television special. That same year, he walked off with a record-breaking eight Grammy awards. Throughout the 1980s, Michael Jackson reigned as the single most popular entertainer in the

— *Michael Jackson* —

world. He packed huge stadiums from the United States to Europe, Africa, and Asia.

Being home alone has never made any kid famous—except **Macaulay Culkin.** "Mac" (as he is called by his fans) was born into a theatrical family. His aunt, father, and three of his five siblings all are professional actors. Macaulay began his career acting in commercials at the age of four. After some bit parts in movies, he landed his first major role in *Uncle Buck*, co-starring with John Candy. Then Culkin was chosen to star in *Home Alone*. Released in 1990, it became a runaway success, the top-grossing comedy of all time.

Life quickly changed for Macaulay. He was spotted by his fans everywhere he went. He continued his education, kept hanging out with his friends, and tried to lead a normal life. But his fame, and his massive fortune, eventually contributed to a disastrous family life. His parents separated, and they staged a long and bitter custody fight over their children.

Another child star who encountered trouble was **River Phoenix**. Born in an Oregon log cabin, River spent his childhood traveling the world with his parents, who were religious missionaries. River caught the

— *Macaulay Culkin* —

acting bug when he was a young teen, and he landed roles in the films *Explorers*, *Stand By Me*, and *Little Nikita*. He won widespread acclaim for his acting in *My Own Private Idaho* (1991). But as with so many other famous youths, River had trouble turning the corner to adulthood. He had a restless temper and used dangerous drugs. In 1993, River died of a drug overdose, shocking his family, friends, and many fans.

— *River Phoenix* —

— *Sarah Jessica Parker in costume as Annie* —

— *Ron Howard (right) on "The Andy Griffith Show"*—

Many child stars, however, mature into happy and successful adults who continue their careers in show business. **Sarah Jessica Parker** starred in the title role of the hit Broadway show *Annie*. After that role ended, Sarah left the spotlight for several years. She returned as a major adult movie star in the 1990s with starring roles in *L.A. Story* and *Honeymoon in Vegas*.

Ron Howard virtually grew up on television. For years, he starred as little Opie, the cute, red-headed son on "The Andy Griffith Show." As a teenager, Ron starred on yet another show that was the most popular of its time—"Happy Days." Although Ron Howard's acting days ended in the 1970s, he still lives happy days as one of the most successful film directors in America. His films *Cocoon*,

— *Jodie Foster with her 1988 Best Actress Oscar®* —

Backdraft, and *Apollo 13* are some of the biggest-grossing films in history.

Another young actor-turned-director is **Jodie Foster**. Like so many other actors, Jodie spent years doing commercials while she wanted to land leading roles in movies. When she was twelve, she shocked audiences with her gritty and disturbing performance in the violent film *Taxi Driver*. In many ways, the tough-girl role fit Jodie perfectly. She continued her successful acting career into adulthood, and she won an Academy Award for her performance in *The Accused*. Today, Jodie splits her time between acting and directing major motion pictures. She has formed her own production company, and she is considered one of the most respected and powerful women in Hollywood.

RYAN JAMES
SOCIAL REFORMER AT AGE THIRTEEN
1975–

AIDS is one of the most devastating diseases known today. People with AIDS experience a roller coaster of symptoms that keep them weak and frequently in the hospital. Society treats many people with AIDS like outcasts.

For some AIDS patients, their only companions are their house pets. But they are often unable to care for these animals on their own. Ryan James helped found a program that provides loving animal care to pets owned by people who have AIDS. What began as an Eagle Scout project turned into a long-term fund-raising effort that helps dying people who have few places to turn.

Ryan and his mother, Ellen James, lived with a dog and four cats in their Irving, Texas, home. At the time Ryan began his program, he was in eighth grade at a local middle school, and he enjoyed swimming, skating, and scouting. Before he could become an Eagle Scout in the Boy Scouts, Ryan needed to complete a community project. He had to prove he could create, plan, and lead others in a service program that served the community.

Ryan's mother suggested that he do something for people with AIDS. Ellen knew many AIDS patients through her work as a nurse at the county hospital. "After talking with some AIDS patients, I decided to combine my interests in caring for animals with my desire to help people with AIDS," Ryan says.

To learn more about AIDS, Ryan contacted the AIDS Resource Center in Dallas. The coordinator suggested that Ryan go through a volunteer training program. During this program, Ryan met other workers who walked dogs or found homes for pets of patients who were too ill to care for their animals. After many discussions, Ryan and these volunteers created Pet Pals.

Pet Pals supplied food, veterinary care, grooming, and walking—whatever the pets' owners could not provide on their own. In addition, the group offered information, support, and financial assistance to patients so they could keep their pets at home. If someone entered the hospital or died, Pet Pals secured foster care or adoptive homes for his or her pets.

Because Ryan was too young to drive, he tackled the job of fund-raising to support Pet Pals activities. At first, he asked local merchants to donate pet food, cat litter, veterinary care, and other necessities. Then Ryan thought of writing to celebrities. Actress Whoopi Goldberg thought Ryan had a wonderful program. Her manager suggested that Ryan raise money through an auction of items autographed by celebrities. Ryan wrote letters and received autographed items from such celebrities as Lily Tomlin, John Glenn, and Michael Keaton. "Razzle Dazzle," the celebrity auction, became an annual event in Dallas.

Two years after Pet Pals began, the organization enlisted more than forty volunteers to help about seventy-five people with AIDS. Ryan's contribution expanded beyond letter writing. He spent hundreds of hours on additional fund-raisers, such as a haunted house, a dog show, and a dog birthday party.

These outstanding achievements earned Ryan his Eagle Scout badge. In fact, he became something of a celebrity himself. Every Dallas newspaper carried a story about Ryan, Pet Pals, and the celebrity auctions. In 1989 and 1990, Ryan was honored as the Volunteer of the Year by the Dallas Volunteer Center and a local television station. In 1990, Ryan earned the J.C. Penney Golden Rule Award and the Bronze Congressional Award for volunteer service. When the book *You Can Do Something About AIDS* was revised, the author asked Ryan to write a chapter about Pet Pals. This gave Ryan an opportunity to get other young people involved in helping people with AIDS. "This is no longer just an Eagle Scout project," emphasizes Ryan. "I have become fully committed to the program."

WANG YANI
ARTIST AT AGE SIX
1975–

Fang Shiqiang refused to take his young daughter's artwork seriously. The two-year-old girl liked to draw on anything, even on the walls of Shiqiang's art studio. She imitated the way her father (who was an artist) cocked his head and stood back to observe his oil paintings. Shiqiang found Yani's imitations amusing—that is, until she scribbled on a picture he had just completed.

When her father got angry, proud little Yani dissolved into tears. "Daddy," she sobbed, "I want to paint like you!" The words reminded Shiqiang of his own childhood, when he longed for pencil, paper, and someone to teach him to draw. But his parents only punished him for messing up his room. Shiqiang vowed that his daughter would have the chance to paint that he had wanted as a child.

Shiqiang gave Yani her own paper and brushes. The youngster eagerly painted flowers, pine trees, and animals. To Shiqiang's surprise, Yani progressed quickly with her drawing. She possessed a special gift for painting creative images. But Shiqiang decided not to give Yani formal training. He wanted to free her imagination to paint whatever and however she wished. Shiqiang encouraged Yani to explore her own style through trial and error.

By the time Yani was eight years old, Shiqiang gave up painting to keep his work from influencing her style. He believed his job was to guide his young daughter. He took Yani to zoos, gardens, and other places that would add to her visual experiences.

Yani was particularly fascinated by the animals she saw, especially monkeys. The lively creatures served as Yani's favorite subjects to draw for many years. As Yani got older, her animals took on more human qualities, emotions usually captured by more experienced artists.

Yani's brightly colored pictures attracted the interest of several Chinese artists. One painter from her native province of Guangxi sent some of her pictures to a friend at the Shanghai Art School. Artists in Shanghai were so taken by her expressive characters that they arranged for Yani to have a solo park exhibit and to give demonstrations at the International Club. These demonstrations gave the young artist visibility within her own country, as well as among foreign diplomats.

By age six, Yani had created four thousand watercolor and ink drawings. She received national honors for collections exhibited in major Chinese cities and in Hong Kong. Yani gained international fame for her lively art through exhibitions in Japan, West Germany, and England.

In 1989, Yani toured the United States and became the youngest artist ever to exhibit at the Smithsonian Institution in Washington, D.C. Visitors to the show were impressed with her wide-eyed, playful figures, lotus flowers, and winding rivers. What many enjoyed most, however, was seeing the barefoot artist in shorts drawing to music. She used splotches and heavy brush strokes to make simple trees with blossoms and branches, recording her zest for life in rapid brush strokes for all to see.

By age sixteen, Yani drew fewer lively animals. Instead, she painted calmer scenes of nature that surrounded her hometown. Yani's parents never sold her paintings, so the family lived modestly. Her mother continued to sell toys at a department store. Yani attended the local high school with other kids her age.

Meanwhile, Yani continued drawing, even under the watchful eyes of the art world. Critics followed her progress closely. They wondered if her remarkable talents would continue into adulthood.

Yani, a girl who preferred paintbrushes to friends, is thoughtful about her progress. In a 1995 interview, she advised, "Don't be afraid of what others will say about you. Just express your own ideas. Enjoy yourself."

TIGER WOODS
GOLF CHAMPION AT AGE FIVE
1976–

arl and Kultida Woods suspected that their son had athletic ability when he was only ten months old. While most babies that age need to have balls rolled to them, little Eldrick could hit a whiffle ball with a bat!

When Eldrick was eleven months old, he sat for two hours watching his father hit golf balls into a net in the garage. Then Earl left the garage for a few minutes. When he returned, Earl saw his son imitate the way he set up balls and held a club. The biggest surprise came when Eldrick swung the club several times and hit the balls into the net.

Earl Woods took the youngster to a golf course near their Cypress, California, home. He told Eldrick to hit some balls into a hole to test his son's golf talent. Earl soon discovered that Eldrick possessed the coordination to learn this adult game.

Earl taught Eldrick how to stand and hit the ball. He explained what different golf terms meant. Terms such as "reverse weight transfer," "over the top," and "set up" became Eldrick's first words when he began to talk. Soon, swinging a golf club was as natural to Eldrick as walking was to other preschool children. The youngster was so quick to learn that he reminded his father of a commander Earl had known during the Vietnam War. "He was a tiger on the field, and my son is a tiger on the course," Earl said. The nickname stuck, and Eldrick became known as "Tiger" Woods.

Tiger loved everything about golf. He enjoyed toy cars and trucks, but his favorite toys were golf equipment. Tiger liked other sports, but loved swinging the clubs on a golf course. Tiger often called his father at work, begging him to come home and take him to the golf course for practice.

By the time Tiger entered kindergarten, he had been competing in junior tournaments for two years. He even had a professional coach. Using special clubs that fit his short body, he won many trophies playing against golfers who were more than three times his age. Teenagers were often embarrassed losing to someone so young.

News of the boy with unusual golf abilities traveled. Tiger appeared on television talk shows and in newspaper articles. The media have followed Tiger's progress since he was two years old.

At school, Tiger was a regular guy. He made friends easily, and teachers found him exceptionally bright. At one point, a teacher wanted to place Tiger in an advanced class. Tiger objected. He spent so much time on the golf course with older people that he liked being with children his own age at school.

As Tiger grew, his interest in golf deepened. He loved the pressure of playing against opponents who played better than he did. During summers, Tiger practiced three or four days a week. The rest of the week and over school holidays, he played in tournaments.

By age fourteen, Tiger was playing forty to forty-five tournaments a year. Whenever he was not in school, he practiced golf. The Woods family traveled to golf courses in Thailand, France, and the United States to watch Tiger compete. Tiger won five world junior championships, and the Professional Golfing Association (PGA) ranked him as the second-best amateur in the world.

Over the next five years, Tiger became the only three-time winner of the U.S. Junior Amateur championship. In 1995, he stole the show at the prestigious Masters golf tournament. Tiger was the only amateur to play in the tournament, and he held his own among professional players who had been playing for decades.

The sports world eagerly waited for Tiger to turn professional and join the PGA tour. But the cool young golfer insisted that before he goes pro, he must finish his college education at Stanford University. Meanwhile, his young fans can attend one of the many golf clinics for young African-Americans that Tiger has organized around the country.

TONY ALIENGENA
RECORD-SETTING PILOT AT AGE NINE
1978–

Flying had been an important part of Tony Aliengena's life since the age of three. He accompanied his father on flights in the family's Cessna 210 airplane. Sometimes, Tony's father allowed Tony to steer the plane. Anyone is allowed to fly a plane as long as there is a licensed pilot on board.

When Tony was nine years old, he saw a television news report about an eleven-year-old boy who was the youngest person to fly across the United States. "I can do that. I can beat that kid's record," Tony told his father.

At first, his father thought the idea was a passing fancy that soon would be forgotten. But Tony never forgot. He kept asking his parents about flying cross-country. Finally, they were convinced he was serious about taking up the challenge.

Tony added three to five weekly flying lessons to his schedule, which was already full with school and baseball. Tony was a good math student and had great powers of concentration. These qualities are important in learning to fly a plane. When he earned forty hours of flying time, Tony was ready to fly solo. Federal Aviation Administration (FAA) rules prohibited anyone under sixteen from flying alone in planes under FAA control. Tony sidestepped the regulation by taking his first solo flight in an ultra-light aircraft, a model outside FAA ruling. With only two minutes in the air, Tony became the youngest person on record to pilot a plane alone.

For the next two months, Tony prepared for his historic flight. While on spring break from school, Tony boarded the single-engine Cessna with his father, an instructor, an observer from the National Aeronautic Association, a local reporter, and a photographer. The group made eight stops in ten days, soaring across the United States.

On the trip east, Tony braved some unexpected difficulties. The plane hit a bad storm and bumped its way from Memphis to Chattanooga, Tennessee. Tony became airsick in the storm. The weather was so bad that Tony's instructor took over the controls for a while. Tony had to fly that stretch of the flight again, or the trip would not have been approved. Fortunately, the rest of the trip went well.

Tony landed in San Juan Capistrano after flying about 6,000 miles (9,656 km). He was greeted by an excited crowd and dozens of reporters. Tony had reached his goal of being the youngest pilot to fly coast to coast.

Before the excitement of his flight wore off, Tony began planning something even bigger and better. He wanted to fly around the world.

First, Tony and his father planned their route. They figured out how far the Cessna could fly before it needed refueling. Then, Tony wrote to foreign governments and asked for permission to fly across their countries. When he received the necessary approvals, Tony and his family began raising money to finance their adventure.

Tony decided to call his trip Friendship Flight '89. He and his family talked about presenting a friendship scroll to the Soviet people when they landed in the Soviet Union. They sent letters to thousands of American schoolchildren inviting them to sign the scroll. Schools that decided to participate received a piece of the scroll to sign and mail back to the Aliengenas. Tony and his family then glued the pieces together. By the time it was completed, the scroll included almost a quarter of a million signatures and stretched nearly 1,000 feet (305 m). In addition to the scroll, Tony organized a pen pal program between the United States and the Soviet Union.

In the summer of 1989, Tony began his 21,537-mile (34,661-km) journey around the world. He was joined by his father as copilot, and his mother and younger sister as passengers. The Aliengenas completed the trip in forty-eight days, making thirty-six stops.

One of Tony's most memorable stops was in the Soviet Union. Soviet representatives officially welcomed the pilot at a ceremony in Moscow. There, Tony presented the signed scroll and a bag of letters to Soviet children. In exchange, the Soviets gave Tony a scroll, signed by Soviet children, for Tony to deliver to U.S. president George Bush. Tony returned home as the youngest pilot to fly a plane around the world.

JASON GAES
AUTHOR OF HOPE AT AGE EIGHT
1978–

If you get cansur don't be scared cause lots of people get over having cansur and grow up without dying. Like Mike Nelson and Doug Cerny and Vince Varpness and President Reagan and me.

—Jason Gaes

After a two-year battle with cancer, eight-year-old Jason Gaes included this message of hope in a children's book that he wrote. Although his future was uncertain at the time, Jason reached out to others who had serious illnesses.

Until Jason was six, his life was similar to that of many boys and girls. He lived in Worthington, Minnesota, with his parents and siblings. He went to kindergarten and enjoyed playing sports and visiting his grandmother. During one summer visit, Jason's uncle noticed a lump in the boy's mouth. Jason's mother took him to a dentist to remove the lump. Jason's life was never the same.

The lump was a growth from a form of cancer, a disease in which unhealthy body cells attack and destroy healthy ones. With Jason's cancer, the lumps, called tumors, grew quickly and attacked different parts of his body. Doctors told Jason's parents that their son had little chance of living until his seventh birthday.

Jason went through many types of tests and treatments to rid his body of cancer. Some were very painful. Others made him sick and exhausted and caused his hair to fall out. After six months of constant treatment, Jason wanted to quit going to doctors. His mother promised him anything if he would continue. She wanted her son to live. Jason agreed to stay in treatment if he could have "the biggest party in the world" when it ended.

A year later, Jason still was having blood tests and receiving medicine through a needle at the end of a tube called an IV (intravenous). When he was in the hospital, many well-wishers sent cards and gifts. Jason also received a book about a boy with cancer. He compared his experiences to those of the boy in the story, except for the ending—the boy in the book died. "Why don't they write about kids who live and grow up?" he complained to his mother. Geralyn Gaes suggested that Jason write his own book.

Jason took six months to pull his ideas together for the book. At first, he talked into a tape recorder, pretending to be a child who just learned he had cancer. Then he wrote the story in book form. Jason's brothers drew pictures to help explain the story. Jason wanted boys and girls with cancer to know what to expect. There would be some good things, like presents and no school, and some pretty awful and scary times, too. Jason even added his telephone number and address in case readers wanted to contact him. They could talk or cry or write—whatever made them feel better. Jason's book was called *My book for kids with cansur*.

Two years after Jason's ordeal began, he gave copies of his completed, hand-bound book to each of five hundred friends and relatives at the party that celebrated his triumph over cancer. News of the book and the unselfish boy who wrote it spread to local newspapers and television. A publisher agreed to print a hardbound version just as Jason and his brothers had created it. Now healthy and sick children all over the world can read about Jason's courageous battle with cancer. They could also learn about his dream to help sick children after he becomes a "doctor who takes care of kids with cansur."

After doctors pronounced Jason cured, he and his family agreed to devote their time and energy to reducing the pain of cancer for other families. Jason was interviewed on most major talk shows and in every leading magazine. He spoke to schoolchildren who had cancer and to groups of adults, such as doctors, nurses, and social workers who treat children with cancer. Jason's schedule became so filled with speaking engagements he needed a tutor to help him keep his above-average grades at school. His family set aside one day every week to sort and answer the thirty to three hundred letters that Jason received weekly. And every night, he answered several calls from kids asking what it is like to have cancer.

Jason's work earned him the American Courage Award from President Ronald Reagan in 1988. Publishers translated his book into many foreign languages, including Japanese, German, and French, and a Dutch record was produced based on the story. In 1989, Jason and his family reenacted the portion of their lives that dealt with cancer in the film *You Don't Have to Die*. The film won a 1989 Academy Award for best documentary. Four years later, the Gaes family published the book *You Don't Have to Die: One Family's Guide to Surviving Cancer*. The book and film helped many families to deal with their child's health crisis. More important, Jason proved that kids with cancer "don't always die."

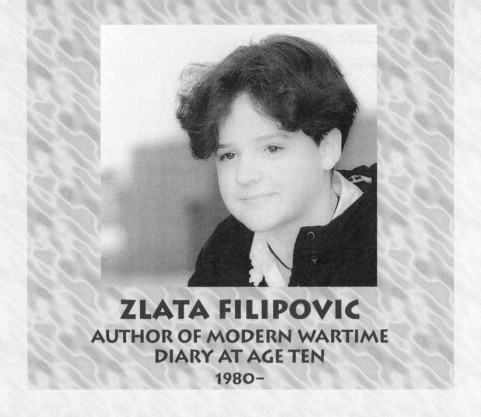

ZLATA FILIPOVIC
AUTHOR OF MODERN WARTIME
DIARY AT AGE TEN
1980–

On September 2, 1991, ten-year-old Zlata Filipovic began her two-year diary. Every few days, she entered notes about key events in her happy life. Within six months, however, diary entries revealed frightening changes in Sarajevo, the city in Yugoslavia where Zlata lived. What began as fond memories turned into another retelling of war's horrors, similar to Anne Frank's diary.

At first, Zlata recounted tales of carefree days. Like many kids, she delighted in eating pizza and skiing with her parents. She loved birthday parties and considered joining a fan club for the American rock singer, Madonna. Most of her diary entries concerned school, piano playing, tennis, and hanging out with friends.

Zlata never discussed government or racial prejudice in these cheerful writings. There was no need. To Zlata, good people were good people, whether they were Muslims, Serbians, or Croatians—the three main ethnic groups in Yugoslavia.

In December 1991, the republics of Bosnia and Herzegovina declared independence from Yugoslavia. Fighting erupted in nearby towns. The conflict still was far from Zlata's life, however. She continued writing about sleepovers and ski trips.

By March 1992, Bosnians had voted to form an independent state. The Serbian minority, which included government leaders and the military, demanded the right to carve out a separate territory for themselves. Suddenly, it mattered whether a family was Muslim, Serbian, or Croatian. Bosnian was pitted against Bosnian.

Violence soon spread to Sarajevo, shattering Zlata's untroubled life. First, the shelling started. Zlata saw bombs destroy buildings, gardens, and then lives. Breadlines formed as food shortages developed. Snipers fired at innocent people. One of Zlata's friends was shot and killed in a city park.

Because of the snipers and shelling, being outdoors grew dangerous. Zlata's school closed, and her music and tennis lessons stopped. The war isolated Zlata at home. She couldn't even enter certain rooms in her house because random gunshots might break through windows at anytime.

Throughout the ordeal, Zlata wrote in her diary. She often scolded politicians for acting like "kids" who tried "to outwit each other" at ordinary people's expense. Zlata wrote:

> *The "kids" are playing, which is why us kids are not playing, we are living in fear, we are not enjoying the sun and flowers, we are not enjoying our childhood. WE ARE CRYING.*

The war dragged on. Friends and family fled to safer countries. But Zlata's father could not leave. Instead, her family stayed without water, electricity, and gas for months at a time. Before the war, Zlata's mother was a chemist, and her father was a lawyer. Now, her mother carried buckets of water when it was safe to go outside. Her father chopped furniture into firewood to warm the family against the frigid winter. Reaching the depths of despair, Zlata wrote:

> BOREDOM!!! SHOOTING!!! SHELLING!!! PEOPLE BEING KILLED!!! DESPAIR!!! HUNGER!!! MISERY!!! FEAR!!! That's my life! The life of an innocent eleven-year-old schoolgirl!! A schoolgirl without a school. . . . A child without games, without friends, without the sun, without birds, without nature. . . . In short, a child without a childhood.

One fall day a year after she began her diary, Zlata's teacher visited her. Zlata told her about the diary, and the teacher said she knew that UNICEF wanted to publish a child's diary to show the world how war hurts innocent children.

Zlata carefully rewrote sample pages and submitted them to UNICEF. The diary was accepted and made into a book. It first appeared in Zlata's Croat language. Almost immediately, the book attracted attention from media around the world.

A French publisher printed *Zlata's Diary*. Advertisements called the author the "Anne Frank of Sarajevo." Before publication, Zlata had connected her misfortune with Anne's. Both girls hid in shelters and struggled with food and supply shortages. Zlata even named her diary "Mimmy," after a dead goldfish, because Anne Frank had called her diary "Kitty." But Zlata grew uncomfortable with the constant comparison to Anne Frank—a girl who had suffered so greatly and eventually died.

Zlata's future soon brightened. The publishers pushed French authorities to help Zlata and her parents escape Sarajevo. The printed diary ended on October 13, 1993. Two months later, Zlata's family resettled in Paris.

A United States publisher purchased the English rights to Zlata's writings. This publisher arranged a whirlwind book-signing tour for Zlata. By the time the tour ended, *Zlata's Diary* was an international best-seller. A Hollywood studio bought the rights to make Zlata's story into a movie.

Zlata had mixed feelings about her sudden fame. She longed for a regular childhood, and she still grieved for friends who lived far away or had died. But her book and its success also brought hope. Zlata's family and publishers donated part of their profits to assist children who still were trapped in war-torn Sarajevo. Moreover, Zlata believed that her book encouraged other people to help Bosnian families. Zlata wanted a happy ending like hers for every child of war.

NAWROSE NUR
WORLD CHESS CHAMPION AT AGE NINE
1981–

Around the world, millions of people play chess. In many countries chess is followed as a major sport. Famous tournaments are held in Europe, Asia, and North and South America. Chess champions work many years to win enough matches to become F.I.D.E. Master, International Master, or Grand Master, three international titles granted by the World Chess Federation. Most serious players begin studying the game at ten to twelve years of age, and they peak when they are in their twenties or thirties. Nawrose Nur attained international status as F.I.D.E. Master at age nine.

Nawrose was born in Dacca, capital of the poor Asian country of Bangladesh. At the time, Nawrose's father, Mohammed, was product manager of a multinational corporation. The job afforded the family advantages that were out of reach for most people in poverty-stricken Dacca. Because of his father's position, Nawrose went to an English school. He learned to speak English, and he received the kind of high-quality education that is unavailable to most Bangladeshi children.

One day, Nawrose's father came home from work with a chessboard and pieces. At first, the curious six-year-old thought the pieces were toys. His mother quickly stopped him from throwing the little men around the room and pretending they were soldiers. Soon Nawrose began watching his mother and father play the game. He showed such interest that his father taught him how to play.

To Mohammed's surprise, Nawrose quickly grasped the complex rules. He did so well that Mohammed hired a coach and bought whatever books he could find to encourage his son's talents. Meanwhile, Nawrose remained fascinated by the pieces and the strategies behind moving them. He progressed with unusual speed. The coach told Mohammed that his son showed great potential.

Within six months, Mohammed entered Nawrose in local competition. There the youngster changed before his father's eyes. The normally quiet boy played with strong determination to win. He easily defeated adults who were four and five times his age. Some games lasted as long as five hours, but Nawrose concentrated throughout every match.

By age seven, Nawrose was the youngest chess champion in Bangladesh. For the next year, he traveled to many foreign countries, representing Bangladesh in chess tournaments. In London, Nawrose won the title of World Chess Champion of players under ten. Nawrose continued his success by winning matches in Puerto Rico, Bulgaria, Romania, Kuwait, and the Soviet Union. He either was champion or placed very high against other children and adults in each tournament.

In 1989, Nawrose came to the United States for a tournament. He was thrilled to learn that U.S. children had many opportunities to learn about chess and to play against each other. At home and in countries such as Russia, children were excluded from most tournaments. Mohammed found a job in New York City, and the entire family moved there.

Initially, Nawrose's New York teachers doubted whether he could handle third-grade schoolwork. But the youngster's knowledge of English helped him adapt easily. Nawrose settled into his classroom within a couple of weeks, making friends and learning to enjoy American comic books and cartoons. Soon his daily routines were much the same as in Dacca. Every day after school, Nawrose completed his homework and practiced chess for three to five hours. For fun, he worked out tricky chess moves on his computer.

Nawrose showed remarkable talent in mathematics. When New York schools tested their students for math, Nawrose scored highest of all third-graders, achieving almost a perfect score. He received honors from the New York Elementary Math Olympic League, the Kodak Corporation, and the *New York Daily News*.

The next summer, Nawrose represented the United States in the World Chess Championship for players under ten. Chess players came from forty-five countries. Nawrose won eight games, tied in three, and lost none. He also won tournaments designed for teenagers! In 1990, he received the title of F.I.D.E. Master. The nine-year-old was the youngest player ever to receive the title.

Nawrose continued winning honors into junior high. In the early 1990s, he won virtually every national chess championship available. And in 1995, Nawrose captured the national high-school chess championship—even though he was still in junior high school! From 1990 to 1995, Nawrose was named to the All-American chess team by the American Chess Federation.

Young Nawrose takes these honors in stride. Despite a busy schedule, he continues to maintain top grades. He excels in science, math, and computer science. Yet he has his sites set on greater goals. Besides his desire to do medical research, Nawrose strives to become chess champion of the world.

GLOSSARY

acacia tree — a small tree or shrub

AIDS (Acquired Immunodeficiency Syndrome) — an incurable disease that attacks the immune system

amateur — unpaid, generally considered on a lower level than professional

ambassador — a person who officially represents a country's government in a foreign nation

anorexia — disease in which a person resorts to starving to keep from gaining weight

Apollo Theater — famous theater in Harlem, New York, which is a showcase for African-American entertainment talent

apprentice — a person (usually young) who works with and assists a professional or craftsperson

architect — a person who designs and oversees the construction of buildings

aria — a song from an opera sung by a solo voice and accompanied by an instrument or orchestra

ballerina — a female ballet dancer

boarding school — a school where the students go to live and study

bobbin — a cylinder or spindle on which yarn or thread is wound

broncobuster — a person who trains wild horses

Burgundians — a group of French people who supported the English army in France against the power of the French king in the twelfth century

cannery — a factory where food is sealed in cans

choreographer — a person who plans how dancers will move about during a dance performance

chronometer — a timepiece designed to keep time very accurately

classical mythology — tales from ancient Greece and Rome

clavier — a keyboard instrument similar to today's piano that was popular at the end of the eighteenth century

clergy — people trained to be priests, ministers, rabbis, and other religious leaders

Cold War (1945–1989) — struggle for power between the United States and the Soviet Union in which the threat of nuclear war was present for several decades

concentration camp — a place where a large number of people are imprisoned without legal proceedings

concert pianist — a classical piano player who makes a living by performing for audiences

concerto — a musical piece in which a solo instrument is accompanied by an orchestra

conductor — the person who guides an orchestra or band

conservatory — a school where musicians learn to read, write, and play music

crossfire — random shots fired from both sides during a battle

Cupid — mythical boy angel who causes people to fall in love by shooting them with a magical bow and arrow

Depression (or the Great Depression) — a period of severe economic hardship that began in 1929 and ended with the onset of World War II in 1939

diplomat — a person who conducts negotiations between nations

dormitory — a building where students sleep and eat meals while attending school

drive-by shooting — the act of shooting a person from a moving automobile

Eagle Scout — the highest rank in the Boy Scouts of America

etching — a picture made by scraping a design on a hard, flat surface

Euclid — Greek philosopher who developed the first concepts of geometry

Federal Aviation Administration (FAA) — government agency that oversees air travel in the United States

Federal Communications Commission (FCC) — government agency that regulates radio and television communication in the United States

fencing — a sport in which contestants duel with swords

finishing school — school that prepares students for higher professional school

flogging — a punishment in which a person is whipped

food rationing — a system of conserving food in which every person is allowed a certain amount of food

formal education — learning that occurs in schools and with teachers

ghetto — a place where people in an ethnic group or at a lower economic level are isolated from the larger community

gimlet — a small tool with a handle and a screw point

Golden Gloves — the major amateur boxing tournament in the United States

gristmill — a mill where grain is ground into flour

ham radio — another name for amateur radio

hemophilia — a disease in which the blood cannot clot to block wounds

Industrial Revolution — a period beginning in the late eighteenth century when many people who had lived and worked on farms went to work in large factories in cities

Juilliard School of Music — a prestigious music school in New York City

loom — a machine that weaves thread into cloth

lumber mill — a building where cut trees are processed into lumber and paper products

luxury — something that is often expensive and is not necessary to survival

lynching — when a group of people decide to execute someone, usually by hanging, without the consent of the law

March of Dimes — a charitable organization that raises money to help fight birth defects

medieval — related to the Middle Ages (A.D. 800–1400)

moonwalk —a dance step in which a person glides across the floor in the opposite direction that one's feet are moving.

Morse code — communication system in which long and short sounds representing letters of words are transmitted

Muslim — a member of the Islamic religion

National Association for the Advancement of Colored People (NAACP) — an organization that promotes the economic, political, and social progress of African-Americans

National Gallery — a museum in Great Britain that houses some of the greatest works of art in the world

national guard — military units called to active duty in times of war or emergency

nobility — the class of people who possess privilege and wealth in European society

opera — a musical drama in which singers are accompanied by an orchestra

patent — an official document that gives an inventor full rights to his or her invention

payroll — a list of a company's paid workers

pen pal — a friend who is made and kept by writing letters

perfect pitch — the ability to recognize or sing any musical note

pesticide — a chemical used to kill insects or germs

philosopher — a person who studies the history of human thought and develops original ideas

poorhouse — an 1800s term referring to a place where poor people go for shelter

Pre-Raphaelite Brotherhood — a group of English artists from the 19th century who wanted painters to return to the style used before the 16th-century Italian painter Raphael

preparatory school — a private school that prepares teenage students for college

prima ballerina — an Italian phrase for the lead female dancer in a ballet company

prima donna — an Italian phrase for the lead female singer in an opera company

prodigy — a person who is extremely talented at a very young age

professional — a person who is paid to perform a task

quill — a pen made out of a feather, used during the eighteenth century

quiz show — a radio or television program in which contestants win prizes by answering questions of general knowledge

realism — a philosophy stating that art should imitate the real world as closely as possible

Red Cross — organization created to supply relief in regions that have suffered a disaster

Redcoats — name given to soldiers of the English army who fought the American colonists during the Revolutionary War

rhythm-and-blues — musical style originated by African-Americans in the South during the late 1800s

rooming house — a place where traveling people rent a room

rotary engine — an engine in which power is harnessed through parts that move in circles

saint — a person who is officially recognized as holy by the church

scholarship — financial support for a student to pay the expenses of schooling

secondary school — the school between elementary school and college (commonly called "high school" in the United States)

secretary of labor — government official who oversees the job economy in the United States

secretary of state — government official who conducts relations with foreign governments

sextant — a tool that measures angles; used to locate one's position at sea by measuring the position of stars

shuttle — a weaving device used to make cloth

sight-read — to play a piece of music while reading the music for the first time

Smithsonian Institution — several museums and research centers in Washington, D.C., supported by the U.S. government

soprano — the singer in a choir or opera who sings the highest notes

Soviet Union (Union of Soviet Socialist Republics, or USSR) — a federation of socialist states that was a major world power from 1917 to 1989

steppe — a vast, level, treeless area in southeastern Europe and Asia

stonecutter — a person who earns a living by cutting stone for use in construction and art

stop-motion device — a special mechanism that automatically stops a machine in case of emergency to prevent injuries to workers

symphony — a musical piece in which an entire orchestra performs

Tatars — a group of Turkish people found mainly in Eastern Asia

Texas Ranger — a law-enforcement official who patrolled the border between Texas and Mexico during the 1840s

track-and-field sports — events that take place on a running track and in the field inside the track; includes such sports as running races, hurdles, long jump, high jump, and shot put.

transcontinental — anything (such as a railroad) that stretches across the entire continent

transfusion — the process by which a body receives extra blood from an outside source through tubes

tuberculosis — a bacterial disease that attacks the lungs

typhus — a bacterial disease that causes a high fever and death

UNICEF (United Nations International Children's Emergency Fund)—an organization created to supply food and assistance to children suffering from war or hunger

Union Army — the Northern army in the American Civil War

United Nations — an international organization that provides nations with a forum to resolve their differences peacefully

university — a place of learning, research, teaching, and scholarship

vaudeville — stage entertainment popular in the early 1900s in which a variety of acts were performed in one show

ventriloquist — a person who can speak without moving his or her lips, giving the impression that a puppet (or "dummy") is speaking

victory garden — a garden planted by people during World War II to increase food production

whaling — the act of hunting whales

World Cup — a soccer tournament held every four years in which the world's best national teams compete

writer's block — a condition in which a writer cannot free his or her imagination and write anything of quality

Wunderkind — a German phrase meaning "wonder child" used to describe a child who is extraordinarily talented

yoke — a wooden bar or frame by which two draft animals are joined together

FOR FURTHER INFORMATION

BOOKS

Aaseng, Nathan. *Jim Henson, Muppet Master*. Minneapolis: Lerner Publications, 1988.

Altman, Susan. *Extraordinary Black Americans*. Chicago: Children's Press, 1989.

Alyson, Sasha. *You Can Do Something About AIDS*. Boston: The Stop AIDS Project, 1988.

Arnold, Caroline. *Pelé: The King of Soccer*. New York: Franklin Watts, 1992.

Beals, Melba Pattillo. *Warriors Don't Cry*. New York: Avon, 1994.

Brill, Marlene Targ. *Allen Jay and the Underground Railroad*. Minneapolis: Carolrhoda Books, 1993.

Brown, Drollene. *Sybil Rides For Independence*. Niles, IL: A. Whitman, 1985.

Bryant, Jennifer. *Louis Braille*. New York: Chelsea House, 1993.

Carmer, Carl. *A Cavalcade of Young Americans*. New York: Lothrop, Lee & Shepard, 1958.

Christopher, Tracy. *Joan of Arc*. New York: Chelsea House, 1993.

Coecho, Tony. *John Quincy Adams*. New York: Chelsea House, 1990.

Daly, Jay. *Presenting S. E. Hinton*. Boston: Twayne Publishers, 1987.

de Monvel, Boutet. *Joan of Arc*. New York: The Pierpont Morgan Library and The Viking Press, 1980.

DiCerto, Joseph J. *Pony Express: Hoofbeats in the Wilderness*. New York: Franklin Watts, 1989.

Filipovic, Zlata. *Zlata's Diary*. New York: Viking, 1994.

Frank, Anne. *The Diary of a Young Girl*. New York: Random House, 1952.

Gaes, Jason. *My book for kids with cansur*. Aberdeen, SD: Melius & Peterson Publishing, 1987.

Glockner, Carolyn. *Sugar Ray Leonard*. Mankato, MN: Crestwood House, 1985.

Gormaly, Beatrice. *Maria Mitchell: The Soul of an Astronomer*. Grand Rapids, MI: W.B. Eerdmans, 1995.

Greene, Laura. *Child Labor: Then and Now.* New York: Franklin Watts, 1992.

Gridley, Marion. *Maria Tallchief: The Story of an American Indian.* Minneapolis: Dillon Press, 1973.

Haskins, James. *Pelé: A Biography.* Garden City, New York: Doubleday, 1976.

Haskins, James. *Shirley Temple Black, Actress to Ambassador.* New York: Viking Penguin, 1988.

Henry, Marguerite. *Benjamin West and His Cat Grimalkin.* New York: Macmillan, 1987.

Kudinski, Kathleen. *Rachel Carson, Pioneer of Ecology.* New York: Viking Kestrel, 1988.

Levine, Ellen. *Freedom's Children.* New York: Avon, 1993.

Loeper, John. *Going to School in 1876.* New York: Atheneum, 1984.

Markham, Lois. *Helen Keller.* New York: Franklin Watts, 1993

Rambeck, Richard. *Wayne Gretzky.* Plymouth, MN: Child's World, 1995.

Smith, Samantha. *Journey to the Soviet Union.* Boston: Little, Brown and Company, 1985.

Thames, Richard. *Wolfgang Amadeus Mozart.* New York: Franklin Watts, 1991.

Venezia, Mike. *Michelangelo.* Chicago: Children's Press, 1991.

Venezia, Mike. *Mozart.* Chicago: Children's Press, 1995.

Ventura, Piero. *Michelangelo's World.* New York: G. P. Putman's Sons, 1989.

ORGANIZATIONS

National Boy Scouts of America
1325 Walnut Hill Lane, Irving, Texas 75038

Pony Express Museum
914 Penn Street, St. Joseph, Missouri 64501

Samantha Smith Foundation
9 Union Street, Hallowell, Maine 04347

Teens on Target/Youth Alive
3012 Summit Avenue, Suite 3570
Summit Medical Center
Oakland, California 94609

INDEX

ABOUT THE AUTHOR

Marlene Targ Brill has written more than twenty-five books for children and adults. She particularly likes to write about amazing successes of everyday people. Her credits include *John Adams, James Buchanan, Guatemala,* and *Building the Capital City* for Children's Press; *Journey for Peace: The Story of Rigoberta Menchu* for Lodestar; and *Allen Jay and the Underground Railroad* for Carolrhoda, which came from research for *Extraordinary Young People.* Marlene lives in the Chicago area with husband Richard, daughter Alison, and mischievous poodle Fluffy.

ABOUT THE DESIGNER

Lindaanne Donohoe is a designer-illustrator who has worked for several book publishers. She has designed and electronically produced several popular series for Children's Press: *Encyclopedia of Presidents, The World's Great Explorers,* and *Extraordinary People.* She is also the proud parent of daughter Nicole, and lives in Chicago, Illinois.